C-227 CAREER EXAMINATION SERIES

This is your
PASSBOOK for...

Electronic Equipment Maintainer

Test Preparation Study Guide
Questions & Answers

COPYRIGHT NOTICE

This book is SOLELY intended for, is sold ONLY to, and its use is RESTRICTED to individual, bona fide applicants or candidates who qualify by virtue of having seriously filed applications for appropriate license, certificate, professional and/or promotional advancement, higher school matriculation, scholarship, or other legitimate requirements of education and/or governmental authorities.

This book is NOT intended for use, class instruction, tutoring, training, duplication, copying, reprinting, excerption, or adaptation, etc., by:

1) Other publishers
2) Proprietors and/or Instructors of "Coaching" and/or Preparatory Courses
3) Personnel and/or Training Divisions of commercial, industrial, and governmental organizations
4) Schools, colleges, or universities and/or their departments and staffs, including teachers and other personnel
5) Testing Agencies or Bureaus
6) Study groups which seek by the purchase of a single volume to copy and/or duplicate and/or adapt this material for use by the group as a whole without having purchased individual volumes for each of the members of the group
7) Et al.

Such persons would be in violation of appropriate Federal and State statutes.

PROVISION OF LICENSING AGREEMENTS – Recognized educational, commercial, industrial, and governmental institutions and organizations, and others legitimately engaged in educational pursuits, including training, testing, and measurement activities, may address request for a licensing agreement to the copyright owners, who will determine whether, and under what conditions, including fees and charges, the materials in this book may be used them. In other words, a licensing facility exists for the legitimate use of the material in this book on other than an individual basis. However, it is asseverated and affirmed here that the material in this book CANNOT be used without the receipt of the express permission of such a licensing agreement from the Publishers. Inquiries re licensing should be addressed to the company, attention rights and permissions department.

All rights reserved, including the right of reproduction in whole or in part, in any form or by any means, electronic or mechanical, including photocopying, recording, or by any information storage and retrieval system, without permission in writing from the Publisher.

Copyright © 2024 by
National Learning Corporation

212 Michael Drive, Syosset, NY 11791
(516) 921-8888 • www.passbooks.com
E-mail: info@passbooks.com

PUBLISHED IN THE UNITED STATES OF AMERICA

PASSBOOK® SERIES

THE *PASSBOOK® SERIES* has been created to prepare applicants and candidates for the ultimate academic battlefield – the examination room.

At some time in our lives, each and every one of us may be required to take an examination – for validation, matriculation, admission, qualification, registration, certification, or licensure.

Based on the assumption that every applicant or candidate has met the basic formal educational standards, has taken the required number of courses, and read the necessary texts, the *PASSBOOK® SERIES* furnishes the one special preparation which may assure passing with confidence, instead of failing with insecurity. Examination questions – together with answers – are furnished as the basic vehicle for study so that the mysteries of the examination and its compounding difficulties may be eliminated or diminished by a sure method.

This book is meant to help you pass your examination provided that you qualify and are serious in your objective.

The entire field is reviewed through the huge store of content information which is succinctly presented through a provocative and challenging approach – the question-and-answer method.

A climate of success is established by furnishing the correct answers at the end of each test.

You soon learn to recognize types of questions, forms of questions, and patterns of questioning. You may even begin to anticipate expected outcomes.

You perceive that many questions are repeated or adapted so that you can gain acute insights, which may enable you to score many sure points.

You learn how to confront new questions, or types of questions, and to attack them confidently and work out the correct answers.

You note objectives and emphases, and recognize pitfalls and dangers, so that you may make positive educational adjustments.

Moreover, you are kept fully informed in relation to new concepts, methods, practices, and directions in the field.

You discover that you are actually taking the examination all the time: you are preparing for the examination by "taking" an examination, not by reading extraneous and/or supererogatory textbooks.

In short, this PASSBOOK®, used directedly, should be an important factor in helping you to pass your test.

ELECTRONIC EQUIPMENT MAINTAINER

DUTIES:
Electronic Equipment Maintainers, under supervision, maintain, install, inspect, test, alter and repair electronic wireless and wired communication systems, and digital and analog control equipment and systems in the shop or in the field, including radio systems, closed circuit video equipment, and other electronic communication equipment; perform circuit testing, analysis, and fault identification; keep records; operate motor vehicles; and perform related work.

THE TEST:
The qualifying multiple-choice test may include questions on basic electronic and electrical theory; proper selection and use of tools, instruments and materials; safe, proper and efficient work practices; reading and interpreting electrical schematics; and other related areas.

The competitive practical skills test may require you to perform tasks related to the installation, testing, maintenance and repair of electronic and electrical communications equipment, including the proper use of hand tools, meters and other testing equipment, and safe work practices and procedures.

HOW TO TAKE A TEST

I. YOU MUST PASS AN EXAMINATION

A. WHAT EVERY CANDIDATE SHOULD KNOW

Examination applicants often ask us for help in preparing for the written test. What can I study in advance? What kinds of questions will be asked? How will the test be given? How will the papers be graded?

As an applicant for a civil service examination, you may be wondering about some of these things. Our purpose here is to suggest effective methods of advance study and to describe civil service examinations.

Your chances for success on this examination can be increased if you know how to prepare. Those "pre-examination jitters" can be reduced if you know what to expect. You can even experience an adventure in good citizenship if you know why civil service exams are given.

B. WHY ARE CIVIL SERVICE EXAMINATIONS GIVEN?

Civil service examinations are important to you in two ways. As a citizen, you want public jobs filled by employees who know how to do their work. As a job seeker, you want a fair chance to compete for that job on an equal footing with other candidates. The best-known means of accomplishing this two-fold goal is the competitive examination.

Exams are widely publicized throughout the nation. They may be administered for jobs in federal, state, city, municipal, town or village governments or agencies.

Any citizen may apply, with some limitations, such as the age or residence of applicants. Your experience and education may be reviewed to see whether you meet the requirements for the particular examination. When these requirements exist, they are reasonable and applied consistently to all applicants. Thus, a competitive examination may cause you some uneasiness now, but it is your privilege and safeguard.

C. HOW ARE CIVIL SERVICE EXAMS DEVELOPED?

Examinations are carefully written by trained technicians who are specialists in the field known as "psychological measurement," in consultation with recognized authorities in the field of work that the test will cover. These experts recommend the subject matter areas or skills to be tested; only those knowledges or skills important to your success on the job are included. The most reliable books and source materials available are used as references. Together, the experts and technicians judge the difficulty level of the questions.

Test technicians know how to phrase questions so that the problem is clearly stated. Their ethics do not permit "trick" or "catch" questions. Questions may have been tried out on sample groups, or subjected to statistical analysis, to determine their usefulness.

Written tests are often used in combination with performance tests, ratings of training and experience, and oral interviews. All of these measures combine to form the best-known means of finding the right person for the right job.

II. HOW TO PASS THE WRITTEN TEST

A. NATURE OF THE EXAMINATION

To prepare intelligently for civil service examinations, you should know how they differ from school examinations you have taken. In school you were assigned certain definite pages to read or subjects to cover. The examination questions were quite detailed and usually emphasized memory. Civil service exams, on the other hand, try to discover your present ability to perform the duties of a position, plus your potentiality to learn these duties. In other words, a civil service exam attempts to predict how successful you will be. Questions cover such a broad area that they cannot be as minute and detailed as school exam questions.

In the public service similar kinds of work, or positions, are grouped together in one "class." This process is known as *position-classification*. All the positions in a class are paid according to the salary range for that class. One class title covers all of these positions, and they are all tested by the same examination.

B. FOUR BASIC STEPS

1) Study the announcement

How, then, can you know what subjects to study? Our best answer is: "Learn as much as possible about the class of positions for which you've applied." The exam will test the knowledge, skills and abilities needed to do the work.

Your most valuable source of information about the position you want is the official exam announcement. This announcement lists the training and experience qualifications. Check these standards and apply only if you come reasonably close to meeting them.

The brief description of the position in the examination announcement offers some clues to the subjects which will be tested. Think about the job itself. Review the duties in your mind. Can you perform them, or are there some in which you are rusty? Fill in the blank spots in your preparation.

Many jurisdictions preview the written test in the exam announcement by including a section called "Knowledge and Abilities Required," "Scope of the Examination," or some similar heading. Here you will find out specifically what fields will be tested.

2) Review your own background

Once you learn in general what the position is all about, and what you need to know to do the work, ask yourself which subjects you already know fairly well and which need improvement. You may wonder whether to concentrate on improving your strong areas or on building some background in your fields of weakness. When the announcement has specified "some knowledge" or "considerable knowledge," or has used adjectives like "beginning principles of..." or "advanced ... methods," you can get a clue as to the number and difficulty of questions to be asked in any given field. More questions, and hence broader coverage, would be included for those subjects which are more important in the work. Now weigh your strengths and weaknesses against the job requirements and prepare accordingly.

3) Determine the level of the position

Another way to tell how intensively you should prepare is to understand the level of the job for which you are applying. Is it the entering level? In other words, is this the position in which beginners in a field of work are hired? Or is it an intermediate or advanced level? Sometimes this is indicated by such words as "Junior" or "Senior" in the class title. Other jurisdictions use Roman numerals to designate the level – Clerk I, Clerk II, for example. The word "Supervisor" sometimes appears in the title. If the level is not indicated by the title, check the description of duties. Will you be working under very close supervision, or will you have responsibility for independent decisions in this work?

4) Choose appropriate study materials

Now that you know the subjects to be examined and the relative amount of each subject to be covered, you can choose suitable study materials. For beginning level jobs, or even advanced ones, if you have a pronounced weakness in some aspect of your training, read a modern, standard textbook in that field. Be sure it is up to date and has general coverage. Such books are normally available at your library, and the librarian will be glad to help you locate one. For entry-level positions, questions of appropriate difficulty are chosen – neither highly advanced questions, nor those too simple. Such questions require careful thought but not advanced training.

If the position for which you are applying is technical or advanced, you will read more advanced, specialized material. If you are already familiar with the basic principles of your field, elementary textbooks would waste your time. Concentrate on advanced textbooks and technical periodicals. Think through the concepts and review difficult problems in your field.

These are all general sources. You can get more ideas on your own initiative, following these leads. For example, training manuals and publications of the government agency which employs workers in your field can be useful, particularly for technical and professional positions. A letter or visit to the government department involved may result in more specific study suggestions, and certainly will provide you with a more definite idea of the exact nature of the position you are seeking.

III. KINDS OF TESTS

Tests are used for purposes other than measuring knowledge and ability to perform specified duties. For some positions, it is equally important to test ability to make adjustments to new situations or to profit from training. In others, basic mental abilities not dependent on information are essential. Questions which test these things may not appear as pertinent to the duties of the position as those which test for knowledge and information. Yet they are often highly important parts of a fair examination. For very general questions, it is almost impossible to help you direct your study efforts. What we can do is to point out some of the more common of these general abilities needed in public service positions and describe some typical questions.

1) General information

Broad, general information has been found useful for predicting job success in some kinds of work. This is tested in a variety of ways, from vocabulary lists to questions about current events. Basic background in some field of work, such as sociology or economics, may be sampled in a group of questions. Often these are principles which have become familiar to most persons through exposure rather than through formal training. It is difficult to advise you how to study for these questions; being alert to the world around you is our best suggestion.

2) Verbal ability

An example of an ability needed in many positions is verbal or language ability. Verbal ability is, in brief, the ability to use and understand words. Vocabulary and grammar tests are typical measures of this ability. Reading comprehension or paragraph interpretation questions are common in many kinds of civil service tests. You are given a paragraph of written material and asked to find its central meaning.

3) Numerical ability

Number skills can be tested by the familiar arithmetic problem, by checking paired lists of numbers to see which are alike and which are different, or by interpreting charts and graphs. In the latter test, a graph may be printed in the test booklet which you are asked to use as the basis for answering questions.

4) Observation

A popular test for law-enforcement positions is the observation test. A picture is shown to you for several minutes, then taken away. Questions about the picture test your ability to observe both details and larger elements.

5) Following directions

In many positions in the public service, the employee must be able to carry out written instructions dependably and accurately. You may be given a chart with several columns, each column listing a variety of information. The questions require you to carry out directions involving the information given in the chart.

6) Skills and aptitudes

Performance tests effectively measure some manual skills and aptitudes. When the skill is one in which you are trained, such as typing or shorthand, you can practice. These tests are often very much like those given in business school or high school courses. For many of the other skills and aptitudes, however, no short-time preparation can be made. Skills and abilities natural to you or that you have developed throughout your lifetime are being tested.

Many of the general questions just described provide all the data needed to answer the questions and ask you to use your reasoning ability to find the answers. Your best preparation for these tests, as well as for tests of facts and ideas, is to be at your physical and mental best. You, no doubt, have your own methods of getting into an exam-taking mood and keeping "in shape." The next section lists some ideas on this subject.

IV. KINDS OF QUESTIONS

Only rarely is the "essay" question, which you answer in narrative form, used in civil service tests. Civil service tests are usually of the short-answer type. Full instructions for answering these questions will be given to you at the examination. But in case this is your first experience with short-answer questions and separate answer sheets, here is what you need to know:

1) **Multiple-choice Questions**

Most popular of the short-answer questions is the "multiple choice" or "best answer" question. It can be used, for example, to test for factual knowledge, ability to solve problems or judgment in meeting situations found at work.

A multiple-choice question is normally one of three types—
- It can begin with an incomplete statement followed by several possible endings. You are to find the one ending which *best* completes the statement, although some of the others may not be entirely wrong.
- It can also be a complete statement in the form of a question which is answered by choosing one of the statements listed.

- It can be in the form of a problem – again you select the best answer.

Here is an example of a multiple-choice question with a discussion which should give you some clues as to the method for choosing the right answer:

When an employee has a complaint about his assignment, the action which will *best* help him overcome his difficulty is to
- A. discuss his difficulty with his coworkers
- B. take the problem to the head of the organization
- C. take the problem to the person who gave him the assignment
- D. say nothing to anyone about his complaint

In answering this question, you should study each of the choices to find which is best. Consider choice "A" – Certainly an employee may discuss his complaint with fellow employees, but no change or improvement can result, and the complaint remains unresolved. Choice "B" is a poor choice since the head of the organization probably does not know what assignment you have been given, and taking your problem to him is known as "going over the head" of the supervisor. The supervisor, or person who made the assignment, is the person who can clarify it or correct any injustice. Choice "C" is, therefore, correct. To say nothing, as in choice "D," is unwise. Supervisors have and interest in knowing the problems employees are facing, and the employee is seeking a solution to his problem.

2) True/False Questions

The "true/false" or "right/wrong" form of question is sometimes used. Here a complete statement is given. Your job is to decide whether the statement is right or wrong.

SAMPLE: A roaming cell-phone call to a nearby city costs less than a non-roaming call to a distant city.

This statement is wrong, or false, since roaming calls are more expensive.

This is not a complete list of all possible question forms, although most of the others are variations of these common types. You will always get complete directions for answering questions. Be sure you understand *how* to mark your answers – ask questions until you do.

V. RECORDING YOUR ANSWERS

Computer terminals are used more and more today for many different kinds of exams.

For an examination with very few applicants, you may be told to record your answers in the test booklet itself. Separate answer sheets are much more common. If this separate answer sheet is to be scored by machine – and this is often the case – it is highly important that you mark your answers correctly in order to get credit.

An electronic scoring machine is often used in civil service offices because of the speed with which papers can be scored. Machine-scored answer sheets must be marked with a pencil, which will be given to you. This pencil has a high graphite content which responds to the electronic scoring machine. As a matter of fact, stray dots may register as answers, so do not let your pencil rest on the answer sheet while you are pondering the correct answer. Also, if your pencil lead breaks or is otherwise defective, ask for another.

Since the answer sheet will be dropped in a slot in the scoring machine, be careful not to bend the corners or get the paper crumpled.

The answer sheet normally has five vertical columns of numbers, with 30 numbers to a column. These numbers correspond to the question numbers in your test booklet. After each number, going across the page are four or five pairs of dotted lines. These short dotted lines have small letters or numbers above them. The first two pairs may also have a "T" or "F" above the letters. This indicates that the first two pairs only are to be used if the questions are of the true-false type. If the questions are multiple choice, disregard the "T" and "F" and pay attention only to the small letters or numbers.

Answer your questions in the manner of the sample that follows:

32. The largest city in the United States is
    A. Washington, D.C.
    B. New York City
    C. Chicago
    D. Detroit
    E. San Francisco

1) Choose the answer you think is best. (New York City is the largest, so "B" is correct.)
2) Find the row of dotted lines numbered the same as the question you are answering. (Find row number 32)
3) Find the pair of dotted lines corresponding to the answer. (Find the pair of lines under the mark "B.")
4) Make a solid black mark between the dotted lines.

VI. BEFORE THE TEST

Common sense will help you find procedures to follow to get ready for an examination. Too many of us, however, overlook these sensible measures. Indeed, nervousness and fatigue have been found to be the most serious reasons why applicants fail to do their best on civil service tests. Here is a list of reminders:

- Begin your preparation early – Don't wait until the last minute to go scurrying around for books and materials or to find out what the position is all about.
- Prepare continuously – An hour a night for a week is better than an all-night cram session. This has been definitely established. What is more, a night a week for a month will return better dividends than crowding your study into a shorter period of time.
- Locate the place of the exam – You have been sent a notice telling you when and where to report for the examination. If the location is in a different town or otherwise unfamiliar to you, it would be well to inquire the best route and learn something about the building.
- Relax the night before the test – Allow your mind to rest. Do not study at all that night. Plan some mild recreation or diversion; then go to bed early and get a good night's sleep.
- Get up early enough to make a leisurely trip to the place for the test – This way unforeseen events, traffic snarls, unfamiliar buildings, etc. will not upset you.
- Dress comfortably – A written test is not a fashion show. You will be known by number and not by name, so wear something comfortable.

- Leave excess paraphernalia at home – Shopping bags and odd bundles will get in your way. You need bring only the items mentioned in the official notice you received; usually everything you need is provided. Do not bring reference books to the exam. They will only confuse those last minutes and be taken away from you when in the test room.
- Arrive somewhat ahead of time – If because of transportation schedules you must get there very early, bring a newspaper or magazine to take your mind off yourself while waiting.
- Locate the examination room – When you have found the proper room, you will be directed to the seat or part of the room where you will sit. Sometimes you are given a sheet of instructions to read while you are waiting. Do not fill out any forms until you are told to do so; just read them and be prepared.
- Relax and prepare to listen to the instructions
- If you have any physical problem that may keep you from doing your best, be sure to tell the test administrator. If you are sick or in poor health, you really cannot do your best on the exam. You can come back and take the test some other time.

VII. AT THE TEST

The day of the test is here and you have the test booklet in your hand. The temptation to get going is very strong. Caution! There is more to success than knowing the right answers. You must know how to identify your papers and understand variations in the type of short-answer question used in this particular examination. Follow these suggestions for maximum results from your efforts:

1) Cooperate with the monitor

The test administrator has a duty to create a situation in which you can be as much at ease as possible. He will give instructions, tell you when to begin, check to see that you are marking your answer sheet correctly, and so on. He is not there to guard you, although he will see that your competitors do not take unfair advantage. He wants to help you do your best.

2) Listen to all instructions

Don't jump the gun! Wait until you understand all directions. In most civil service tests you get more time than you need to answer the questions. So don't be in a hurry. Read each word of instructions until you clearly understand the meaning. Study the examples, listen to all announcements and follow directions. Ask questions if you do not understand what to do.

3) Identify your papers

Civil service exams are usually identified by number only. You will be assigned a number; you must not put your name on your test papers. Be sure to copy your number correctly. Since more than one exam may be given, copy your exact examination title.

4) Plan your time

Unless you are told that a test is a "speed" or "rate of work" test, speed itself is usually not important. Time enough to answer all the questions will be provided, but this does not mean that you have all day. An overall time limit has been set. Divide the total time (in minutes) by the number of questions to determine the approximate time you have for each question.

5) Do not linger over difficult questions

If you come across a difficult question, mark it with a paper clip (useful to have along) and come back to it when you have been through the booklet. One caution if you do this – be sure to skip a number on your answer sheet as well. Check often to be sure that you have not lost your place and that you are marking in the row numbered the same as the question you are answering.

6) Read the questions

Be sure you know what the question asks! Many capable people are unsuccessful because they failed to *read* the questions correctly.

7) Answer all questions

Unless you have been instructed that a penalty will be deducted for incorrect answers, it is better to guess than to omit a question.

8) Speed tests

It is often better NOT to guess on speed tests. It has been found that on timed tests people are tempted to spend the last few seconds before time is called in marking answers at random – without even reading them – in the hope of picking up a few extra points. To discourage this practice, the instructions may warn you that your score will be "corrected" for guessing. That is, a penalty will be applied. The incorrect answers will be deducted from the correct ones, or some other penalty formula will be used.

9) Review your answers

If you finish before time is called, go back to the questions you guessed or omitted to give them further thought. Review other answers if you have time.

10) Return your test materials

If you are ready to leave before others have finished or time is called, take ALL your materials to the monitor and leave quietly. Never take any test material with you. The monitor can discover whose papers are not complete, and taking a test booklet may be grounds for disqualification.

VIII. EXAMINATION TECHNIQUES

1) Read the general instructions carefully. These are usually printed on the first page of the exam booklet. As a rule, these instructions refer to the timing of the examination; the fact that you should not start work until the signal and must stop work at a signal, etc. If there are any *special* instructions, such as a choice of questions to be answered, make sure that you note this instruction carefully.

2) When you are ready to start work on the examination, that is as soon as the signal has been given, read the instructions to each question booklet, underline any key words or phrases, such as *least, best, outline, describe* and the like. In this way you will tend to answer as requested rather than discover on reviewing your paper that you *listed without describing*, that you selected the *worst* choice rather than the *best* choice, etc.

3) If the examination is of the objective or multiple-choice type – that is, each question will also give a series of possible answers: A, B, C or D, and you are called upon to select the best answer and write the letter next to that answer on your answer paper – it is advisable to start answering each question in turn. There may be anywhere from 50 to 100 such questions in the three or four hours allotted and you can see how much time would be taken if you read through all the questions before beginning to answer any. Furthermore, if you come across a question or group of questions which you know would be difficult to answer, it would undoubtedly affect your handling of all the other questions.

4) If the examination is of the essay type and contains but a few questions, it is a moot point as to whether you should read all the questions before starting to answer any one. Of course, if you are given a choice – say five out of seven and the like – then it is essential to read all the questions so you can eliminate the two that are most difficult. If, however, you are asked to answer all the questions, there may be danger in trying to answer the easiest one first because you may find that you will spend too much time on it. The best technique is to answer the first question, then proceed to the second, etc.

5) Time your answers. Before the exam begins, write down the time it started, then add the time allowed for the examination and write down the time it must be completed, then divide the time available somewhat as follows:
    - If 3-1/2 hours are allowed, that would be 210 minutes. If you have 80 objective-type questions, that would be an average of 2-1/2 minutes per question. Allow yourself no more than 2 minutes per question, or a total of 160 minutes, which will permit about 50 minutes to review.
    - If for the time allotment of 210 minutes there are 7 essay questions to answer, that would average about 30 minutes a question. Give yourself only 25 minutes per question so that you have about 35 minutes to review.

6) The most important instruction is to *read each question* and make sure you know what is wanted. The second most important instruction is to *time yourself properly* so that you answer every question. The third most important instruction is to *answer every question*. Guess if you have to but include something for each question. Remember that you will receive no credit for a blank and will probably receive some credit if you write something in answer to an essay question. If you guess a letter – say "B" for a multiple-choice question – you may have guessed right. If you leave a blank as an answer to a multiple-choice question, the examiners may respect your feelings but it will not add a point to your score. Some exams may penalize you for wrong answers, so in such cases *only*, you may not want to guess unless you have some basis for your answer.

7) Suggestions
    a. Objective-type questions
        1. Examine the question booklet for proper sequence of pages and questions
        2. Read all instructions carefully
        3. Skip any question which seems too difficult; return to it after all other questions have been answered
        4. Apportion your time properly; do not spend too much time on any single question or group of questions

5. Note and underline key words – *all, most, fewest, least, best, worst, same, opposite,* etc.
6. Pay particular attention to negatives
7. Note unusual option, e.g., unduly long, short, complex, different or similar in content to the body of the question
8. Observe the use of "hedging" words – *probably, may, most likely,* etc.
9. Make sure that your answer is put next to the same number as the question
10. Do not second-guess unless you have good reason to believe the second answer is definitely more correct
11. Cross out original answer if you decide another answer is more accurate; do not erase until you are ready to hand your paper in
12. Answer all questions; guess unless instructed otherwise
13. Leave time for review

   b. Essay questions
      1. Read each question carefully
      2. Determine exactly what is wanted. Underline key words or phrases.
      3. Decide on outline or paragraph answer
      4. Include many different points and elements unless asked to develop any one or two points or elements
      5. Show impartiality by giving pros and cons unless directed to select one side only
      6. Make and write down any assumptions you find necessary to answer the questions
      7. Watch your English, grammar, punctuation and choice of words
      8. Time your answers; don't crowd material

8) Answering the essay question

Most essay questions can be answered by framing the specific response around several key words or ideas. Here are a few such key words or ideas:

M's: manpower, materials, methods, money, management
P's: purpose, program, policy, plan, procedure, practice, problems, pitfalls, personnel, public relations

   a. Six basic steps in handling problems:
      1. Preliminary plan and background development
      2. Collect information, data and facts
      3. Analyze and interpret information, data and facts
      4. Analyze and develop solutions as well as make recommendations
      5. Prepare report and sell recommendations
      6. Install recommendations and follow up effectiveness

   b. Pitfalls to avoid
      1. *Taking things for granted* – A statement of the situation does not necessarily imply that each of the elements is necessarily true; for example, a complaint may be invalid and biased so that all that can be taken for granted is that a complaint has been registered

2. *Considering only one side of a situation* – Wherever possible, indicate several alternatives and then point out the reasons you selected the best one
3. *Failing to indicate follow up* – Whenever your answer indicates action on your part, make certain that you will take proper follow-up action to see how successful your recommendations, procedures or actions turn out to be
4. *Taking too long in answering any single question* – Remember to time your answers properly

IX. AFTER THE TEST

Scoring procedures differ in detail among civil service jurisdictions although the general principles are the same. Whether the papers are hand-scored or graded by machine we have described, they are nearly always graded by number. That is, the person who marks the paper knows only the number – never the name – of the applicant. Not until all the papers have been graded will they be matched with names. If other tests, such as training and experience or oral interview ratings have been given, scores will be combined. Different parts of the examination usually have different weights. For example, the written test might count 60 percent of the final grade, and a rating of training and experience 40 percent. In many jurisdictions, veterans will have a certain number of points added to their grades.

After the final grade has been determined, the names are placed in grade order and an eligible list is established. There are various methods for resolving ties between those who get the same final grade – probably the most common is to place first the name of the person whose application was received first. Job offers are made from the eligible list in the order the names appear on it. You will be notified of your grade and your rank as soon as all these computations have been made. This will be done as rapidly as possible.

People who are found to meet the requirements in the announcement are called "eligibles." Their names are put on a list of eligible candidates. An eligible's chances of getting a job depend on how high he stands on this list and how fast agencies are filling jobs from the list.

When a job is to be filled from a list of eligibles, the agency asks for the names of people on the list of eligibles for that job. When the civil service commission receives this request, it sends to the agency the names of the three people highest on this list. Or, if the job to be filled has specialized requirements, the office sends the agency the names of the top three persons who meet these requirements from the general list.

The appointing officer makes a choice from among the three people whose names were sent to him. If the selected person accepts the appointment, the names of the others are put back on the list to be considered for future openings.

That is the rule in hiring from all kinds of eligible lists, whether they are for typist, carpenter, chemist, or something else. For every vacancy, the appointing officer has his choice of any one of the top three eligibles on the list. This explains why the person whose name is on top of the list sometimes does not get an appointment when some of the persons lower on the list do. If the appointing officer chooses the second or third eligible, the No. 1 eligible does not get a job at once, but stays on the list until he is appointed or the list is terminated.

X. HOW TO PASS THE INTERVIEW TEST

The examination for which you applied requires an oral interview test. You have already taken the written test and you are now being called for the interview test – the final part of the formal examination.

You may think that it is not possible to prepare for an interview test and that there are no procedures to follow during an interview. Our purpose is to point out some things you can do in advance that will help you and some good rules to follow and pitfalls to avoid while you are being interviewed.

What is an interview supposed to test?

The written examination is designed to test the technical knowledge and competence of the candidate; the oral is designed to evaluate intangible qualities, not readily measured otherwise, and to establish a list showing the relative fitness of each candidate – as measured against his competitors – for the position sought. Scoring is not on the basis of "right" and "wrong," but on a sliding scale of values ranging from "not passable" to "outstanding." As a matter of fact, it is possible to achieve a relatively low score without a single "incorrect" answer because of evident weakness in the qualities being measured.

Occasionally, an examination may consist entirely of an oral test – either an individual or a group oral. In such cases, information is sought concerning the technical knowledges and abilities of the candidate, since there has been no written examination for this purpose. More commonly, however, an oral test is used to supplement a written examination.

Who conducts interviews?

The composition of oral boards varies among different jurisdictions. In nearly all, a representative of the personnel department serves as chairman. One of the members of the board may be a representative of the department in which the candidate would work. In some cases, "outside experts" are used, and, frequently, a businessman or some other representative of the general public is asked to serve. Labor and management or other special groups may be represented. The aim is to secure the services of experts in the appropriate field.

However the board is composed, it is a good idea (and not at all improper or unethical) to ascertain in advance of the interview who the members are and what groups they represent. When you are introduced to them, you will have some idea of their backgrounds and interests, and at least you will not stutter and stammer over their names.

What should be done before the interview?

While knowledge about the board members is useful and takes some of the surprise element out of the interview, there is other preparation which is more substantive. It *is* possible to prepare for an oral interview – in several ways:

1) Keep a copy of your application and review it carefully before the interview

This may be the only document before the oral board, and the starting point of the interview. Know what education and experience you have listed there, and the sequence and dates of all of it. Sometimes the board will ask you to review the highlights of your experience for them; you should not have to hem and haw doing it.

2) Study the class specification and the examination announcement

Usually, the oral board has one or both of these to guide them. The qualities, characteristics or knowledges required by the position sought are stated in these documents. They offer valuable clues as to the nature of the oral interview. For example, if the job involves supervisory responsibilities, the announcement will usually indicate that knowledge of modern supervisory methods and the qualifications of the candidate as a supervisor will be tested. If so, you can expect such questions, frequently in the form of a hypothetical situation which you are expected to solve. NEVER go into an oral without knowledge of the duties and responsibilities of the job you seek.

3) Think through each qualification required

Try to visualize the kind of questions you would ask if you were a board member. How well could you answer them? Try especially to appraise your own knowledge and background in each area, *measured against the job sought*, and identify any areas in which you are weak. Be critical and realistic – do not flatter yourself.

4) Do some general reading in areas in which you feel you may be weak

For example, if the job involves supervision and your past experience has NOT, some general reading in supervisory methods and practices, particularly in the field of human relations, might be useful. Do NOT study agency procedures or detailed manuals. The oral board will be testing your understanding and capacity, not your memory.

5) Get a good night's sleep and watch your general health and mental attitude

You will want a clear head at the interview. Take care of a cold or any other minor ailment, and of course, no hangovers.

What should be done on the day of the interview?

Now comes the day of the interview itself. Give yourself plenty of time to get there. Plan to arrive somewhat ahead of the scheduled time, particularly if your appointment is in the fore part of the day. If a previous candidate fails to appear, the board might be ready for you a bit early. By early afternoon an oral board is almost invariably behind schedule if there are many candidates, and you may have to wait. Take along a book or magazine to read, or your application to review, but leave any extraneous material in the waiting room when you go in for your interview. In any event, relax and compose yourself.

The matter of dress is important. The board is forming impressions about you – from your experience, your manners, your attitude, and your appearance. Give your personal appearance careful attention. Dress your best, but not your flashiest. Choose conservative, appropriate clothing, and be sure it is immaculate. This is a business interview, and your appearance should indicate that you regard it as such. Besides, being well groomed and properly dressed will help boost your confidence.

Sooner or later, someone will call your name and escort you into the interview room. *This is it.* From here on you are on your own. It is too late for any more preparation. But remember, you asked for this opportunity to prove your fitness, and you are here because your request was granted.

What happens when you go in?

The usual sequence of events will be as follows: The clerk (who is often the board stenographer) will introduce you to the chairman of the oral board, who will introduce you to the other members of the board. Acknowledge the introductions before you sit down. Do not be surprised if you find a microphone facing you or a stenotypist sitting by. Oral interviews are usually recorded in the event of an appeal or other review.

Usually the chairman of the board will open the interview by reviewing the highlights of your education and work experience from your application – primarily for the benefit of the other members of the board, as well as to get the material into the record. Do not interrupt or comment unless there is an error or significant misinterpretation; if that is the case, do not hesitate. But do not quibble about insignificant matters. Also, he will usually ask you some question about your education, experience or your present job – partly to get you to start talking and to establish the interviewing "rapport." He may start the actual questioning, or turn it over to one of the other members. Frequently, each member undertakes the questioning on a particular area, one in which he is perhaps most competent, so you can expect each member to participate in the examination. Because time is limited, you may also expect some rather abrupt switches in the direction the questioning takes, so do not be upset by it. Normally, a board member will not pursue a single line of questioning unless he discovers a particular strength or weakness.

After each member has participated, the chairman will usually ask whether any member has any further questions, then will ask you if you have anything you wish to add. Unless you are expecting this question, it may floor you. Worse, it may start you off on an extended, extemporaneous speech. The board is not usually seeking more information. The question is principally to offer you a last opportunity to present further qualifications or to indicate that you have nothing to add. So, if you feel that a significant qualification or characteristic has been overlooked, it is proper to point it out in a sentence or so. Do not compliment the board on the thoroughness of their examination – they have been sketchy, and you know it. If you wish, merely say, "No thank you, I have nothing further to add." This is a point where you can "talk yourself out" of a good impression or fail to present an important bit of information. Remember, *you close the interview yourself*.

The chairman will then say, "That is all, Mr. _____, thank you." Do not be startled; the interview is over, and quicker than you think. Thank him, gather your belongings and take your leave. Save your sigh of relief for the other side of the door.

How to put your best foot forward

Throughout this entire process, you may feel that the board individually and collectively is trying to pierce your defenses, seek out your hidden weaknesses and embarrass and confuse you. Actually, this is not true. They are obliged to make an appraisal of your qualifications for the job you are seeking, and they want to see you in your best light. Remember, they must interview all candidates and a non-cooperative candidate may become a failure in spite of their best efforts to bring out his qualifications. Here are 15 suggestions that will help you:

1) Be natural – Keep your attitude confident, not cocky

If you are not confident that you can do the job, do not expect the board to be. Do not apologize for your weaknesses, try to bring out your strong points. The board is interested in a positive, not negative, presentation. Cockiness will antagonize any board member and make him wonder if you are covering up a weakness by a false show of strength.

2) Get comfortable, but don't lounge or sprawl

Sit erectly but not stiffly. A careless posture may lead the board to conclude that you are careless in other things, or at least that you are not impressed by the importance of the occasion. Either conclusion is natural, even if incorrect. Do not fuss with your clothing, a pencil or an ashtray. Your hands may occasionally be useful to emphasize a point; do not let them become a point of distraction.

3) Do not wisecrack or make small talk

This is a serious situation, and your attitude should show that you consider it as such. Further, the time of the board is limited – they do not want to waste it, and neither should you.

4) Do not exaggerate your experience or abilities

In the first place, from information in the application or other interviews and sources, the board may know more about you than you think. Secondly, you probably will not get away with it. An experienced board is rather adept at spotting such a situation, so do not take the chance.

5) If you know a board member, do not make a point of it, yet do not hide it

Certainly you are not fooling him, and probably not the other members of the board. Do not try to take advantage of your acquaintanceship – it will probably do you little good.

6) Do not dominate the interview

Let the board do that. They will give you the clues – do not assume that you have to do all the talking. Realize that the board has a number of questions to ask you, and do not try to take up all the interview time by showing off your extensive knowledge of the answer to the first one.

7) Be attentive

You only have 20 minutes or so, and you should keep your attention at its sharpest throughout. When a member is addressing a problem or question to you, give him your undivided attention. Address your reply principally to him, but do not exclude the other board members.

8) Do not interrupt

A board member may be stating a problem for you to analyze. He will ask you a question when the time comes. Let him state the problem, and wait for the question.

9) Make sure you understand the question

Do not try to answer until you are sure what the question is. If it is not clear, restate it in your own words or ask the board member to clarify it for you. However, do not haggle about minor elements.

10) Reply promptly but not hastily

A common entry on oral board rating sheets is "candidate responded readily," or "candidate hesitated in replies." Respond as promptly and quickly as you can, but do not jump to a hasty, ill-considered answer.

11) Do not be peremptory in your answers

A brief answer is proper – but do not fire your answer back. That is a losing game from your point of view. The board member can probably ask questions much faster than you can answer them.

12) Do not try to create the answer you think the board member wants

He is interested in what kind of mind you have and how it works – not in playing games. Furthermore, he can usually spot this practice and will actually grade you down on it.

13) Do not switch sides in your reply merely to agree with a board member

Frequently, a member will take a contrary position merely to draw you out and to see if you are willing and able to defend your point of view. Do not start a debate, yet do not surrender a good position. If a position is worth taking, it is worth defending.

14) Do not be afraid to admit an error in judgment if you are shown to be wrong

The board knows that you are forced to reply without any opportunity for careful consideration. Your answer may be demonstrably wrong. If so, admit it and get on with the interview.

15) Do not dwell at length on your present job

The opening question may relate to your present assignment. Answer the question but do not go into an extended discussion. You are being examined for a *new* job, not your present one. As a matter of fact, try to phrase ALL your answers in terms of the job for which you are being examined.

Basis of Rating

Probably you will forget most of these "do's" and "don'ts" when you walk into the oral interview room. Even remembering them all will not ensure you a passing grade. Perhaps you did not have the qualifications in the first place. But remembering them will help you to put your best foot forward, without treading on the toes of the board members.

Rumor and popular opinion to the contrary notwithstanding, an oral board wants you to make the best appearance possible. They know you are under pressure – but they also want to see how you respond to it as a guide to what your reaction would be under the pressures of the job you seek. They will be influenced by the degree of poise you display, the personal traits you show and the manner in which you respond.

ABOUT THIS BOOK

This book contains tests divided into Examination Sections. Go through each test, answering every question in the margin. We have also attached a sample answer sheet at the back of the book that can be removed and used. At the end of each test look at the answer key and check your answers. On the ones you got wrong, look at the right answer choice and learn. Do not fill in the answers first. Do not memorize the questions and answers, but understand the answer and principles involved. On your test, the questions will likely be different from the samples. Questions are changed and new ones added. If you understand these past questions you should have success with any changes that arise. Tests may consist of several types of questions. We have additional books on each subject should more study be advisable or necessary for you. Finally, the more you study, the better prepared you will be. This book is intended to be the last thing you study before you walk into the examination room. Prior study of relevant texts is also recommended. NLC publishes some of these in our Fundamental Series. Knowledge and good sense are important factors in passing your exam. Good luck also helps. So now study this Passbook, absorb the material contained within and take that knowledge into the examination. Then do your best to pass that exam.

EXAMINATION SECTION

EXAMINATION SECTION
TEST 1

DIRECTIONS: Each question or incomplete statement is followed by several suggested answers or completions. Select the one that BEST answers the question or completes the statement. *PRINT THE LETTER OF THE CORRECT ANSWER IN THE SPACE AT THE RIGHT.*

1. A piece of equipment listed as drawing 100 watts is plugged into a 24 volt DC circuit. The MINIMUM size fuse which would handle this load is _____ amps.   1.____

    A. 2   B. 3   C. 4   D. 5

2. A resistor of 1000 ohms has 3 milliamperes passing through it. The voltage drop across the resistor is _____ volts.   2.____

    A. 3   B. 6   C. 15   D. 300

3. A certain resistor has three colored bands around it. The one nearest the end is green, the next one is orange, and the next one is red. The value of this register is _____ ohms.   3.____

    A. 74   B. 270   C. 5300   D. 64,000

4. An alternating voltage is applied to a capacitor. As the frequency of this voltage is increased, the impedance of the capacitor   4.____

    A. increases
    B. decreases
    C. remains the same
    D. increases or decreases depending on its construction

5. The one of the following that is NOT a part of a transistor is the   5.____

    A. emitter   B. collector   C. base   D. grid

6. A 0.2 ufd capacitor is connected in series with a 0.1 ufd capacitor. The resultant capacity is _____ ufd.   6.____

    A. 0.067   B. 0.67   C. 0.15   D. 0.3

7. The term *Hertz* means the same as   7.____

    A. degrees Centigrade   B. degrees Fahrenheit
    C. revolutions per minute   D. cycles per second

8. In an electrolytic condenser, the dielectric material is   8.____

    A. mylar   B. aluminum oxide
    C. paper   D. sodium chloride

9. The amount by which a transformer will step up or step down a voltage is determined by its   9.____

    A. inductance   B. resistance
    C. magnetic flux   D. turns ratio

10. The electrolyte in a lead plate storage battery (such as that used in cars) is 10.____

    A. aluminum hydroxide   B. sulfuric acid
    C. hydrochloric acid   D. sodium chloride

11. A diode in an electronic circuit is used to 11.____

    A. amplify   B. oscillate   C. attenuate   D. rectify

12. The MAIN function of a filter in a power supply is to 12.____

    A. increase the voltage
    B. decrease the load
    C. smooth out the peaks of the ripple frequency
    D. protect the power transformer

13. The expression *pH* as applied to a liquid refers to its 13.____

    A. salinity   B. specific gravity
    C. viscosity   D. acidity/alkalinity

14. The speed of a synchronous motor is controlled by 14.____

    A. the voltage applied to it
    B. the frequency of the alternating current applied to it
    C. a mechanical governor
    D. the current it draws

15. The capacitance of a condenser is measured in 15.____

    A. oersteds   B. ohms   C. henrys   D. farads

16. The power lost in a 20-ohm resistor, with 0.25 amperes passing through it, is _____ watts. 16.____

    A. 0.04   B. 0.4   C. 1.25   D. 5

17. When soldering a transistor into a circuit, it is good practice to clamp a pair of long-nosed pliers on the lead between the transistor and the end being soldered. This is done to 17.____

    A. prevent the lead from moving
    B. prevent burning the fingers
    C. ground the transistor
    D. prevent the soldering iron's heat from reaching the transistor

18. The commutator of a motor should 18.____

    A. not be lubricated
    B. be lubricated with light oil
    C. be lubricated with heavy grease
    D. be lubricated with hypoid oil

19. The band of wavelengths of visible light covers 19.____

    A. 20-50 centimeters   B. 10-50 meters
    C. 400-700 millimicrons   D. 400-700 millimeters

20. The heat reaching the earth from the sun is transmitted by 20.____

    A. ions
    B. convection
    C. radiation
    D. cosmic rays

21. A *thermistor* is a 21.____

    A. type of thermometer
    B. high power transistor
    C. water heating device
    D. resistor with a negative temperature coefficient

22. In an AC circuit, the term *power factor* refers to the 22.____

    A. horsepower
    B. BTU per watt
    C. ratio of the resistance to the impedance
    D. kilowatts per horsepower

23. 23.____

    [Circuit diagram: Between points A and B, a 4 ohm resistor in series on top branch, a 6 ohm resistor in series on bottom branch, with 10 ohms, 10 ohms, and 20 ohms resistors shown in parallel in the middle.]

    In the above circuit, the TOTAL resistance between points A and B is _____ ohms.

    A. 5   B. 14   C. 20   D. 45

24. Of the four gases listed below, the one that is NOT an air pollutant is 24.____

    A. carbon dioxide
    B. carbon monoxide
    C. sulfur dioxide
    D. hydrogen sulfide

25. The term *milli-roentgen* refers to a unit of 25.____

    A. x-ray radiation
    B. ultraviolet radiation
    C. reluctance
    D. inductance

26. An AC motor drawing 12 amps is plugged into a 15-amp circuit. The starting surge of the motor, however, is 18 amps. 26.____
    The PROPER type of fuse to be used in this situation is

    A. varistor
    B. thermistor
    C. fast-blow
    D. slow-blow

27. Degrees Kelvin is numerically equal to degrees 27.____

    A. Fahrenheit - 15
    B. Centigrade + 27
    C. Fahrenheit + 135
    D. Centigrade + 273

28. In the term *micromicrofarads*, the prefix *micromicro* means multiply by

    A. 10^6 B. 10^3 C. 10^{-12} D. 10^{-6}

29. One horsepower is equivalent to

    A. 276 joules
    B. 746 kilowatts
    C. 746 watts
    D. 291 calories

30. Laminated iron or steel is generally used instead of solid metal in the construction of the field and armature cores in motors and generators.
    The reason for this is to

    A. reduce eddy current losses
    B. increase the voltage
    C. decrease the flux
    D. reduce the cost

31. The instrument used to measure current flow is called a(n)

    A. wattmeter
    B. voltmeter
    C. ammeter
    D. wavemeter

32. Reversing the polarity of the voltage applied to a mica condenser will

    A. destroy it
    B. increase its capacity
    C. decrease its capacity
    D. have no effect on it

33. The *decibel* is the unit used for expressing

    A. light levels
    B. DC voltage
    C. AC current
    D. the ratio between two quantities of either electrical or sound energy

34. In a three-phase Y-connected AC power system, the voltage from leg to ground is 120 volts.
    The voltage between each pair of hot legs is _____ volts.

    A. 160   B. 180   C. 208   D. 240

35. An hygrometer is an instrument which measures

    A. humidity
    B. temperature
    C. specific gravity
    D. luminosity

36. The impedance ratio of a transformer varies _____ the turns ratio.

    A. directly with
    B. as the square of
    C. as the square root of
    D. inversely with

37. Two resistors are connected in series. The current through these resistors is 3 amperes. Resistance #1 has a value of fifty ohms; resistance #2 has a voltage drop of fifty volts across its terminals.
    The TOTAL impressed voltage (across both resistors) is _____ volts.

    A. 100   B. 150   C. 200   D. 250

38. The piece of equipment that should be used to obtain more than one voltage from a fixed voltage direct current source is a(n) 38._____

   A. multitap transformer
   B. resistance-type voltage divider
   C. autotransformer
   D. copper oxide rectifier

39. The ratio of peak to effective (rms) voltage value of a sine wave is 39._____

   A. 2 to 1   B. 1 to 2   C. .707 to 1   D. 1.414 to 1

40. Two coils are connected in series.
    If there is no mutual inductance between the coils, the TOTAL inductance of the two coils is the _____ inductances. 40._____

   A. sum of the individual
   B. product of the individual
   C. product of the square roots of the two
   D. sum of the squares of the individual

41. The impedance of a coil with zero resistance is called the 41._____

   A. reluctance   B. conductance
   C. inductive reactance D. flux

42. The ratio of the energy stored to the energy lost in a coil over a period of one cycle is called its 42._____

   A. efficiency   B. Q
   C. reactance   D. resistance

43. In a vacuum tube, the current is carried by 43._____

   A. ions   B. neutrons   C. electrons   D. molecules

44. The device used to vary the intensity of an incandescent light on a 120V AC circuit is a 44._____

   A. variable capacitor
   B. silicon controlled rectifier
   C. copper oxide rectifier
   D. rf amplifier

45. High power transistors must be mounted on *heat sinks*. The purpose of the heat sinks is to 45._____

   A. improve voltage regulation
   B. increase the transistors' output
   C. keep the transistors warm
   D. keep the transistors cool

46. The one of the following materials that has the HIGHEST conductivity is 46._____

   A. iron   B. zinc   C. copper   D. silver

47. The unit used to express the alternating current impedance of a circuit is the

   A. mho   B. farad   C. ohm   D. rel

48. A certain resistor has four colored bands on it. The fourth band is gold. This means that the resistor

   A. is wirewound
   B. is non-inductive
   C. has a ± 20% tolerance
   D. has a ± 5% tolerance

49. An amplifier has an output voltage waveform that does not exactly follow that of the input voltage.
    This type of distortion is called _____ distortion.

   A. modular
   B. frequency
   C. resonance
   D. amplitude

50. A parallel circuit, resonant at 1000 khz, has its value of capacity doubled and its value of inductance halved.
    Its resonant frequency now is _____ khz.

   A. 500   B. 1000   C. 1500   D. 2000

KEY (CORRECT ANSWERS)

1. D	11. D	21. D	31. C	41. C
2. A	12. C	22. C	32. D	42. B
3. C	13. D	23. B	33. D	43. C
4. B	14. B	24. A	34. C	44. B
5. D	15. D	25. A	35. A	45. D
6. A	16. C	26. D	36. B	46. D
7. D	17. D	27. D	37. C	47. C
8. B	18. A	28. C	38. B	48. D
9. D	19. C	29. C	39. D	49. D
10. B	20. C	30. A	40. A	50. B

TEST 2

DIRECTIONS: Each question or incomplete statement is followed by several suggested answers or completions. Select the one that BEST answers the question or completes the statement. *PRINT THE LETTER OF THE CORRECT ANSWER IN THE SPACE AT THE RIGHT.*

1. A voltmeter which reads 100V full scale has a specified accuracy of 3%. It is hooked across a circuit and reads 97 volts.
   The TRUE voltage can be assumed to be somewhere between

   A. 96.7 and 97.3   B. 94 and 100
   C. 96.07 and 97.03   D. 95.5 and 98.5

2. The product of 127.2 and .0037 is

   A. 4706.4   B. 470.64   C. .47064   D. .0047064

3. The wind velocity at a certain location was measured four times in a 24-hour period. The readings were 32 mph, 10 mph, 16 mph, and 2 mph.
   The AVERAGE wind velocity for that day was _____ mph.

   A. 24   B. 20   C. 15   D. 13

4. When 280 is divided by .014, the answer is

   A. .002   B. 20   C. 200   D. 20,000

5. The square root of 289 is

   A. 1.7   B. 9.7   C. 17   D. 144.5

6. The watts drawn by a resistive load is to be determined. To do this, a voltmeter (10V full scale) is connected across the load, and an ammeter (10 amps full scale) is connected in series with the load. Both instruments are specified as having 1% (full scale) accuracy. The voltmeter reads 9.2V; the ammeter reads 8.3 amps.
   The MOST valid value for the watts drawn is _____ watts.

   A. 76   B. 76.36   C. 76.4   D. 80

7. The formula for converting degrees Centigrade to degrees Fahrenheit is: $°F = (9/5) \cdot (°C) + 32$.
   A temperature of 25° C is equal to

   A. 102.6° F   B. 85° F   C. 77° F   D. 43° F

8. The prefix *kilo* means

   A. multiply by one million
   B. divide by one million
   C. multiply by one thousand
   D. divide by one hundred

9. 2^8 is equal to

   A. 512   B. 256   C. 124   D. 82

10. The prefix *milli* means

    A. multiply by 100
    B. divide by one thousand
    C. divide by one million
    D. multiply by one million

11. If 1/X = 1/20 + 1/20 + 1/40, the value of X is

    A. .125   B. 8   C. 16   D. 20

12. 2×10^6 multiplied by 4×10^{-6} equals

    A. 8   B. 8×10^{-12} C. 8×10^{12} D. 8×10^3

13. 1 inch equals _____ cm.

    A. 0.62   B. 2.54   C. 3.94   D. 16.2

14. 1 kg equals

    A. 2.2 lbs.   B. 17.3 oz.   C. 0.52 lbs.   D. 12 oz.

15. 1 liter equals

    A. 3.78 quarts
    B. 1.057 quarts
    C. 1.39 pints
    D. .067 gallons

16. A circle has a radius of 10 inches.
    Its circumference is _____ inches.

    A. 72.3   B. 62.8   C. 31.4   D. 25

17. A right angle triangle has sides measuring 3 inches and 4 inches; its hypotenuse is 5 inches.
    The area of this triangle is _____ square inches.

    A. 6   B. 20   C. 15   D. 60

18. A square has an area of 81 square inches.
    The length of each side is _____ inches.

    A. 7.9   B. 9   C. 11   D. 17

19. A bottle contains 11 pints of liquid. To this bottle 1.32 pints is then added.
    This is an increase of

    A. 6%   B. 9%   C. 12%   D. 16%

20. A week ago a storage battery read 12.4V. Today its voltage is 8.1% less.
    Its voltage is now

    A. 11.4   B. 10.8   C. 9.3   D. 10.2

21. The advantage of a vacuum tube voltmeter over a regular voltmeter is that it

    A. operates on batteries
    B. operates on 120V AC
    C. has a low input impedance
    D. has a high input impedance

22. A g_m tube tester measures a vacuum tube's   22.____

    A. capacitance   B. resistance
    C. emission   D. transconductance

23. A cathode ray tube is used in a(n)   23.____

    A. audio amplifier   B. radio frequency amplifier
    C. oscilloscope   D. volt-ohm-milliammeter

24. A voltmeter is described as having *1000 ohms per volt*. The current required to produce   24.____
    full scale deflection is

    A. 1 milliampere   B. 1 ampere
    C. 20 milliamperes   D. 0.05 milliamperes

25. The PRIMARY use of a test oscilloscope is to   25.____

    A. analyze complex waveforms
    B. measure resistance
    C. measure capacitance
    D. measure DC voltages

26. A spectrophotometer is an instrument that measures   26.____

    A. photographic film density
    B. the amount of light of a particular wavelength
    C. the amount of airborne dust
    D. x-ray radiation

27. The test instrument generally known as a *multitester* will measure, among other things,   27.____

    A. temperature   B. beta radiation
    C. AC watts   D. DC milliamperes

28. A lightmeter used in measuring incident light gives readings in   28.____

    A. footcandles   B. candlepower
    C. lumens   D. foot-lamberts

29. A selenium photocell is a type known as photo-   29.____

    A. emissive   B. resistive
    C. voltaic   D. transistive

30. In wiring electronic circuits, the solder GENERALLY used is _____ solder.   30.____

    A. silver   B. acid core
    C. aluminum   D. rosin core

31. An unconscious victim of electric shock should be orally administered   31.____

    A. nothing
    B. coffee
    C. alcohol
    D. aromatic apirits of ammonia

32. Persons operating x-ray equipment should wear

   A. safety goggles
   B. insulating gloves
   C. a lead-coated apron and gloves
   D. a surgical mask

33. Harmful radiation is emitted by the element

   A. neon   B. lithium   C. platinum   D. radium

34. When a victim of electrical shock or near drowning is given artificial respiration and he does not appear to respond, the treatment should continue for at least

   A. four hours   B. fifteen minutes
   C. five minutes   D. fifteen hours

35. A person maintaining high voltage equipment should avoid wearing

   A. long hair
   B. sneakers
   C. rings and metallic watchbands
   D. eyeglasses

36. Portable AC equipment is often equipped with a three-wire cable and a three-prong male plug.
   The reason for this is to prevent

   A. radiation   B. electric shock
   C. oscillation   D. ground currents

37. Smoke is seen issuing from a piece of electronic equipment. The FIRST thing that should be done is to

   A. call the fire department
   B. pour water on it
   C. look for a fire extinguisher
   D. shut off the power

38. A match should not be used when inspecting the electrolyte level in a lead-acid battery because the cells emit

   A. nitrogen   B. hydrogen
   C. carbon dioxide   D. sulfur dioxide

39. A person feels nauseated, his mental capacity has been lowered, and he has a severe throbbing headache. It is suspected that he has been poisoned by gas, but there is no apparent odor.
   The poisonous gas is MOST likely to be

   A. sulfur dioxide   B. hydrogen cyanide
   C. carbon monoxide   D. chlorine

40. The purpose of an interlock on a piece of electronic equipment is to

   A. prevent theft of the vacuum tubes
   B. prevent electrical shock to maintenance personnel
   C. prevent rf radiation
   D. keep the equipment cool

41. An alternating voltage is applied to an inductance.
    As the frequency of the voltage is decreased, the impedance of the inductance

   A. decreases
   B. increases
   C. follows the alternating voltage
   D. remains the same

42. A 0.25 ufd condenser is connected in parallel with a 0.50 ufd condenser.
    The resultant capacity is _____ ufd.

   A. 0.167   B. 0.37   C. 0.75   D. 2.5

43. The electrolyte in a carbon-zinc dry cell is

   A. sulfuric acid   B. ammonium chloride
   C. lithium chloride   D. sodium chloride

44. A 5000-ohm resistor has a voltage of 25 volts applied to it.
    The current drawn by the resistor is

   A. 5 milliamperes   B. 5 amperes
   C. 75 milliamperes   D. 1.25 milliamperes

45. A certain resistor has three colored bands around it.
    The one nearest the end is red, the next one is gray, and the next one is yellow.
    The value of the resistor is

   A. 2.7 megaohms   B. 280,000 ohms
   C. 3270 ohms   D. 449 ohms

Questions 46-50.

DIRECTIONS: Questions 46 through 50 are to be answered on the basis of the following paragraph.

The second half of the twin triode acts as a phase modulator. The rf output of the crystal oscillator is impressed on the phase-modulator grid by means of a blocking condenser. The cathode circuit is provided with a large amount of degeneration by an un-bypassed cathode resistor. Because of this degenerative feedback, the transconductance of the triode is abnormally low, so low that the plate current is affected as much by the direct grid-plate capacitance as by the transconductance. The two effects result in plate current vectors almost 180° apart, and the total plate current is the resultant of the two components. In phase, it will be about 90° removed from the phase of the voltage impressed on the grid.

46. As used in the above paragraph, the word *impressed* means MOST NEARLY 46.___

   A. applied B. blocked C. changed D. detached

47. As used in the above paragraph, the word *components* refers to the 47.___

   A. blocking condenser and cathode resistor
   B. twin triode
   C. plate current vectors
   D. grid-plate capacitance

48. According to the above paragraph, degenerative feedback is obtained by means of 48.___

   A. a crystal oscillator
   B. the plate voltage
   C. an un-bypassed cathode resistor
   D. a blocking condenser

49. According to the above paragraph, the cathode resistor is 49.___

   A. very large
   B. not bypassed
   C. in series with an inductance
   D. shunted by a blocking condenser

50. According to the above paragraph, the phase angle between the grid voltage and the total plate current is APPROXIMATELY 50.___

   A. 180° B. 90° C. 270° D. zero

KEY (CORRECT ANSWERS)

1. B	11. B	21. D	31. A	41. A
2. C	12. C	22. D	32. C	42. C
3. C	13. B	23. C	33. D	43. B
4. D	14. A	24. A	34. A	44. A
5. C	15. B	25. A	35. C	45. B
6. A	16. B	26. B	36. B	46. A
7. C	17. A	27. D	37. D	47. C
8. C	18. B	28. A	38. B	48. C
9. B	19. C	29. C	39. C	49. B
10. B	20. A	30. D	40. B	50. B

EXAMINATION SECTION

TEST 1

DIRECTIONS: Each question or incomplete statement is followed by several suggested answers or completions. Select the one that BEST answers the question or completes the statement. *PRINT THE LETTER OF THE CORRECT ANSWER IN THE SPACE AT THE RIGHT.*

1. If a series circuit consist of an inductor with an inductive reactance of 100 ohms and a resistance of 57.7 ohms, the phase angle between voltage and current will be _____ degrees.
   A. 30   B. 35   C. 55   D. 60

2. Approximately what capacitance value is needed to resonate a 2.5 millihenry coil to 2.146 MHz?
   A. 2.2 picofarads
   B. 2.2 microfarads
   C. 87 picofarads
   D. 87 microfarads

3. The suppressor grid in a vacuum tube RF amplifier circuit
   A. accelerates electron flow to the plate
   B. helps to suppress interference
   C. normally increases and decreases the signal gain by control bias
   D. catches/attracts loose electrons that happen to bounce off the plate

4. The presence of a blue glow in a vacuum tube operated as an audio amplifier
   A. could indicate air or gas in the tube
   B. could indicate RF energy is being generated to cause the blue glow
   C. has no effect on the efficiency of the tube
   D. can be eliminated by reducing the frequency of the input signal

5. A beam power tetrode has beam forming plates between the
   A. control grid and screen grid
   B. cathode and control grid
   C. screen grid and the plate
   D. suppressor grid and the plate

6. The main purpose of a screen grid in a vacuum amplifier tube is to
   A. permit higher amplification
   B. decrease secondary emission
   C. absorb some heat from the plate
   D. provide isolation from signal input to control grid signal input

7. Modern reserve transmitters are solid-state designs and transmit using only A2 modulation. When measuring transmitter center frequency, what precaution must be taken?
   A. Antenna must be grounded to suppress spurious side-lobes.
   B. Modulation must be reduced to zero to eliminate sidebands.
   C. Voltage to the PA must be kept at half-value.
   D. Antenna current must be reduced to about 2.5 uA.

8. Voltage may be expressed by what other expression?
   A. Difference of potential
   B. IF drop
   C. Electromotive force
   D. All of the above

   8.____

9. Amperage may also be known by
   A. electron flow
   B. electron drift
   C. electric current flow
   D. all of the above

   9.____

10. Factors which determine the amplitude of the voltage induced in a conductor which is cutting magnetic lines of force is(are)
    A. flux density
    B. velocity that the conductor cuts the magnetic lines of force
    C. the angle at which the conductor cuts through the magnetic lines of force
    D. all of the above

    10.____

11. An electrical potential may be generated by
    A. varying a magnetic field through a circuit
    B. chemical action
    C. photo-electric action
    D. all of the above

    11.____

12. Ohm's law is stated as
    A. E = IR
    B. I = E/R
    C. R = E/I
    D. all of the above

    12.____

13. The unit of electrical power is
    A. watt
    B. joule per second
    C. both A and B
    D. none of the above

    13.____

14. The unit of conductance is
    A. ohm   B. mho   C. henry   D. ampere

    14.____

15. The unit of inductance is
    A. henry   B. joule   C. coulomb   D. ohm

    15.____

16. The ratio of current through a conductor to the voltage which produces it is
    A. inductance
    B. conductance
    C. resistance
    D. none of the above

    16.____

17. The product of the number of turns and the current in amperes used to describe relative magnitude is
    A. ampere turns
    B. joules per second
    C. push-pull convergence
    D. dissipation collection

    17.____

18. The property of a conductor or coil which causes a voltage to be developed across its terminals when the number of magnetic lines of force in the circuit or coil is changed is
    A. capacitance
    B. inductance
    C. conductance
    D. none of the above

    18.____

19. The charge of electricity which passes a given point in one second when a current of one ampere is flowing is
    A. coulomb
    B. joule
    C. watt
    D. none of the above

    19.____

20. C = capacity in farads. Q = the measure of the quantity of charge of electricity in coulombs. E = the applied voltage. So, Q = CE
    A. determines the quantity of charge in a capacitor
    B. determines the Q of a circuit
    C. both A and B
    D. none of the above

    20.____

21. Resistance is
    A. the quantity which determines power loss or dissipation
    B. the factor of proportionality between voltage and current
    C. measured in ohms
    D. all of the above

    21.____

22. The unit of AC impedance in a circuit is
    A. ohm
    B. mho
    C. joule
    D. none of the above

    22.____

23. The unit of capacitance is
    A. farad
    B. microfarad
    C. coulomb
    D. A and B

    23.____

24. Decibel is
    A. the unit used to express the ratio between two sound power levels
    B. the unit used to express the ratio between two electrical power levels
    C. both A and B
    D. none of the above

    24.____

25. What factors determine the charge stored in a capacitor?
    A. Capacitance of the capacitor
    B. The applied voltage
    C. Both A and B
    D. None of the above

    25.____

26. Ohm's law for AC circuits when I = amperes, E = volts, Z = impedance in volts is
    A. I = E/Z
    B. E = IZ
    C. Z = Z/I
    D. all of the above

    26.____

27. The formula for determining the power in a DC circuit when the voltage and resistance are known is
    A. P = (E squared)R
    B. P = EI
    C. P = (I squared)R
    D. PF = W/IE

    27.____

28. The formula for finding power in a DC circuit when current and resistance are known is
    A. P = EI
    B. P = (I squared)R
    C. PF = W/IE
    D. none of the above

    28.____

29. The formula for finding power in a DC circuit when current and voltage are known is
    A. P = EI
    B. P = (I squared)R
    C. PF = W/IE
    D. none of the above

30. The prefix *kilo* means
    A. to multiply by 1000 whatever quantity follows
    B. to divide by 1000 whatever quantity follows
    C. to add 1000 to whatever quantity follows
    D. none of the above

KEY (CORRECT ANSWERS)

1. D	11. D	21. D
2. A	12. D	22. A
3. D	13. C	23. D
4. A	14. B	24. C
5. C	15. A	25. C
6. A	16. B	26. D
7. B	17. A	27. A
8. D	18. B	28. B
9. D	19. A	29. A
10. D	20. A	30. A

TEST 2

DIRECTIONS: Each question or incomplete statement is followed by several suggested answers or completions. Select the one that BEST answers the question or completes the statement. *PRINT THE LETTER OF THE CORRECT ANSWER IN THE SPACE AT THE RIGHT.*

1. The prefix *micro* means _____ whatever quantity follows. 1.____
   A. divide by 1,000,000
   B. multiply by 1,000,000
   C. add 1,000,000 to
   D. divide by 1,000

2. The factor by which the product of volts and amperes must be multiplied to obtain true power is 2.____
   A. power factor
   B. apparent power
   C. phase angle
   D. none of the above

3. The prefix *meg* means _____ whatever quantity follows. 3.____
   A. multiply by 1,000,000
   B. multiply by 100,000
   C. multiply by 1,000
   D. divide by 1,000,000

4. Factors which influence the resistance of a conductor is(are) 4.____
   A. cross-sectional area
   B. length
   C. temperature
   D. all of the above

5. Halving the cross-sectional area of a conductor will 5.____
   A. double the resistance
   B. half the resistance
   C. not affect the resistance
   D. none of the above

6. Name four conducting materials in order of their conductivity. 6.____
   A. Gold, silver, copper, platinum
   B. Silver, gold, zinc, platinum
   C. Silver, copper, zinc, aluminum
   D. Aluminum, zinc, copper, platinum

7. Good insulators at radio frequencies are 7.____
   A. pyrex, mica
   B. isolantite, steatite, polyethylene
   C. rubber, porcelain
   D. A and B

8. A resistance across which a constant voltage is applied is doubled. What power dissipation will result? 8.____
   A. One-half
   B. One-fourth
   C. Doubled
   D. None of the above

9. The needle of a magnetic compass when placed within a coil carrying an electric current 9.____
   A. will tend to become parallel with the axis of the coil
   B. will point to the north pole end of the coil
   C. will point to the south pole end of the coil
   D. A and B

10. Electrical resistance is measured with a(n) 10.____
    A. ohmmeter   B. wattmeter   C. ammeter   D. voltmeter

11. The sum of all voltage drops around a simple DC circuit, including the 11.____
    source, is
    A. zero   B. insignificant
    C. infinite   D. none of the above

12. If a resistance to which a constant voltage is applied is halved, what power 12.____
    dissipation will result?
    A. Doubled   B. Halved   C. Tripled   D. Same

13. The diameter of a conductor six inches long is doubled. What will be the 13.____
    effect on the resistance?
    A. One-fourth the original value
    B. One-half the original value
    C. The resistance varies inversely with the cross-sectional area of the
       conductor
    D. A and C

14. A minute subdivision of matter having the smallest known unit of negative 14.____
    electrical charge is
    A. electron   B. ion   C. gilbert   D. joule

15. Conductors differ from nonconductors, i.e. 15.____
    A. there are a large number of free electrons in a good conductor
    B. there is a small number of free electrons in a non-conductor
    C. there is an equal amount of free electrons in a good conductor and in a
       non-conductor
    D. A and B

16. Direction of flow of DC electricity in a conductor can be determined by 16.____
    A. a magnetic compass and the left hand rule
    B. a magnetic compass and the right hand rule
    C. connecting an ammeter with marked polarities in series with the circuit
    D. A and C

17. The difference between electrical power and electrical energy is 17.____
    A. electrical power is the rate of doing work by electricity
    B. electrical energy is the ability to accomplish work by electricity
    C. A and B
    D. none of the above

18. A positive temperature coefficient means 18.____
    A. resistance increases as the temperature increases
    B. resistance decreases as the temperature decreases
    C. both A and B
    D. none of the above

3 (#2)

19. A liquid which is capable of conducting electricity, but undergoes decomposition while doing so is
    A. an electrolyte
    B. a ferromagnetic material under the influence of a magnetizing force
    C. equal to the ohmic resistance of the circuit
    D. none of the above

    19.____

20. The effective value of an RF current and the heating value of the current are
    A. the same
    B. effective value divided by two equals the heating value
    C. effective value multiplied by two equals the heating value
    D. none of the above

    20.____

21. One horsepower is
    A. 746 watts
    B. roughly 3/4 kilowatt
    C. corresponds to lifting 550 pounds at the rate of one foot per second
    D. all of the above

    21.____

22. What factors determine the heat generated in a conductor?
    A. It is directly proportional to the resistance.
    B. It is directly proportional to the square of the current.
    C. Both A and B
    D. None of the above

    22.____

23. What is the ratio of peak to average value of a sine wave?
    A. 1.57 to 1   B. 1 to 0.636   C. 1 to 1   D. A and B

    23.____

24. When the current sine wave in a circuit reaches its peak value before the voltage wave,
    A. it is said to have a leading power factor
    B. it is said to have a lagging power factor
    C. it is said to be in phase
    D. none of the above

    24.____

25. An *harmonic* is
    A. a whole multiple of an original frequency
    B. the heating value of an RF current
    C. the internal impedance of a power source
    D. a multiple of the power factor

    25.____

26. Assuming a power source to have a fixed value of internal impedance, maximum power will be transferred to the load when
    A. the load impedance equals the internal impedance of the source
    B. the load impedance is higher than the source impedance
    C. the load impedance is lower than the source impedance
    D. none of the above

    26.____

27. When two sine waves of the same frequency do not reach their maximum or minimum values simultaneously,
    A. a phase difference exists
    B. a phase difference does not exist
    C. the sine waves are out of phase
    D. A and C

    27.____

28. Which method may be used to obtain more than one value of voltage from a fixed DC source?
    A. Use a resistance type voltage divider
    B. Connect voltage regulator tubes of suitable values and tap off the desired output voltage
    C. Both A and B
    D. None of the above

    28.____

29. The conductance (G) of a circuit if 6A flows when 12 VDC is applied is
    A. 0.5 mho
    B. 1.0 mho
    C. 0.25 mho
    D. none of the above

    29.____

30. Two 10W, 500 ohm resistors in parallel will dissipate how many watts?
    A. 20 watts   B. 10 watts   C. 30 watts   D. 40 watts

    30.____

KEY (CORRECT ANSWERS)

1.	A	11.	A	21.	D
2.	A	12.	A	22.	C
3.	A	13.	D	23.	D
4.	D	14.	A	24.	A
5.	A	15.	D	25.	A
6.	B	16.	D	26.	A
7.	D	17.	C	27.	D
8.	A	18.	C	28.	C
9.	D	19.	A	29.	A
10.	A	20.	A	30.	A

EXAMINATION SECTION
TEST 1

DIRECTIONS: Each question or incomplete statement is followed by several suggested answers or completions. Select the one that BEST answers the question or completes the statement. *PRINT THE LETTER OF THE CORRECT ANSWER IN THE SPACE AT THE RIGHT.*

1. A 20 ohm resistor with a current of 0.25A passing through it will dissipate how many watts?   1._____
    A. 10 watts   B. 20 watts   C. 0.025 watts   D. 1.25 watts

2. If the voltage to a circuit is doubled and the resistance is increased to three times the original value, what will be the final current?   2._____
    A. 1/3 the original current   B. 2/3 the original current
    C. 3 times the original current   D. none of the above

3. If a vacuum tube with a filament rating of 0.25A and 5V is operated from a 6 volt battery, what value of resistor is necessary?   3._____
    A. 4 ohms   B. 5 ohms   C. 10 ohms   D. 2 ohms

4. The minimum power dissipation rating of a resistor of 20,000 ohms across a potential of 500V should be   4._____
    A. 25 watts   B. 12.5 watts
    C. 15 watts   D. none of the above

5. The total power dissipation capability of two 10 watt, 500 ohm resistors connected in series is   5._____
    A. 20 watts   B. 10 watts
    C. 5 watts   D. none of the above

6. What is the total power dissipation capability of two 10 watt 500 ohm resistors connected in parallel?   6._____
    A. 20 watts   B. 40 watts
    C. 5 watts   D. none of the above

7. What is the maximum current carrying capacity of a resistor of 5000 ohms, 200 watts?   7._____
    A. 0.2A   B. 2A
    C. 1.2A   D. none of the above

8. What is the total resistance of a parallel circuit consisting of a 10 ohm branch and a 25 ohm branch?   8._____
    A. 6 ohms   B. 10.2 ohms   C. 7.0 ohms   D. 7.14 ohms

2 (#1)

9. The current through two resistors in series is 3A. Resistance #1 is 50 ohms; resistance #2 drops 50V across its terminals. What is the total voltage?
   A. 200V   B. 220V   C. 110V   D. 180V

   9.____

10. An 18 ohm and a 15 ohm resistor are connected in parallel; a 36 ohm resistor is connected in series with this combination; a 22 ohm resistor is connected in parallel with this total combination. The total current is 5A. What current is flowing in the 15 ohm resistor?
    A. 0.908A   B. 1.000A   C. 1.908A   D. 0.809A

    10.____

11. A circuit passes 3A. The internal resistance of the source is 2 ohms. The total resistance is 50 ohms. What is the terminal voltage of the source?
    A. 150V   B. 100V   C. 110V   D. 240V

    11.____

12. A relay coil has 500 ohms resistance and operates on 125 mA. What value of resistance should be connected in series with it to operate from 110 VDC?
    A. 380 ohms
    B. 400 ohms
    C. 200 ohms
    D. None of the above

    12.____

13. Given: Input power to a receiver is 75 watts. How much power does the receiver consume in 24 hours of continuous operation?
    A. 1800 watthours
    B. 1.80 kilowatthours
    C. A and B
    D. None of the above

    13.____

14. The total reactance when two capacitances of equal value are connected in series is
    A. the product of the two individual reactances in ohms
    B. the sum of the two individual reactances in ohms
    C. the difference of the two individual reactances in ohms
    D. none of the above

    14.____

15. A capacitor's charge is stored
    A. upon the inner surface of the capacitor plates
    B. as an electrostatic field which exists in the space between the plates
    C. A and B
    D. none of the above

    15.____

16. The voltage drop across an individual capacitor of a group of capacitors connected in series across an AC source is
    A. inversely proportional to the ratio of the capacitance being considered
    B. inversely proportional to the total capacitance of the combination
    C. directly proportional to the applied voltage across the series combination
    D. all of the above

    16.____

17. What is the total capacitance of the capacitors of 3, 5, and 7 microfarad connected in series?
    A. 14.79 microfarad
    B. 1.479 microfarad
    C. 15 microfarad
    D. none of the above

    17.____

18. If capacitors of 3, 5, and 7 microfarad are connected in parallel, what is the total capacitance? 18.____
    A. 9 microfarad
    B. 15 microfarad
    C. 10 microfarad
    D. 3 microfarad

19. How many capacitors of 400 volts and 2 microfarad each would be necessary to obtain a combination rated at 1600 volts and 1.5 microfarad? 19.____
    A. 10
    B. 12
    C. 14
    D. 16

20. If a turn in an inductor is shorted, 20.____
    A. there will be an increase of induction
    B. there will be a decrease of Q
    C. there will be overheating with possible burnout
    D. all of the above

21. The relationship between the number of turns and the inductance of a coil may be expressed by 21.____
    A. the inductance varies approximately as the square of the number of turns
    B. the inductance varies approximately as the square root of the number of turns
    C. both A and B
    D. none of the above

22. The formula for determining the resonant frequency of a circuit when the inductance and capacitance are known is 22.____
    A. f = 1/(2 pi times the square root of LC)
    B. f = 0.159/(the square root of LC)
    C. both A and B
    D. none of the above

23. The formula for determining the wavelength when the frequency is known is 23.____
    A. Wavelength = 300,000/f kHz
    B. Wavelength = 300,000,000/f Hz
    C. Wavelength = 300/f MHz
    D. all of the above

24. The wavelength of the period of one complete cycle of a radio wave of 0.000,001 second is 24.____
    A. 300M
    B. 3000M
    C. 30M
    D. 70 cm

25. The efficiency of a radio device is 25.____
    A. the ratio of the power input to the power output
    B. the ratio of the useful power output to the power input
    C. the ratio of the minimum power output to the maximum power output
    D. none of the above

26. What is the total impedance of a parallel capacitor and inductor with equal values of reactance?
    A. Infinite total reactance
    B. Zero total reactance
    C. Parallel impedance is resistive and infinite
    D. B and C

27. The total inductance of two coils in parallel without any mutual coupling is
    A. equal to the product of the two inductances divided by their sum
    B. the sum of the individual inductances
    C. zero
    D. none of the above

28. What is the total reactance of a series AC circuit, with no resistance and equal inductance and capacitive reactances?
    A. The two reactances cancel being equal and opposite.
    B. Net impedance is purely resistive and contains no reactive component.
    C. The total impedance is zero at the resonant frequency.
    D. All of the above

29. The total inductance of two coils in series without any mutual coupling is
    A. the sum of the individual inductances
    B. the product of the individual inductances divided by their sum
    C. infinite
    D. none of the above

30. One wave-length is
    A. the distance a wave will travel in the time for one cycle
    B. centimeter wavelength = 30,000/frequency MHz
    C. A and B
    D. neither A nor B

KEY (CORRECT ANSWERS)

1.	D	11.	A	21.	A
2.	B	12.	A	22.	C
3.	A	13.	C	23.	D
4.	A	14.	B	24.	A
5.	A	15.	C	25.	B
6.	A	16.	D	26.	D
7.	A	17.	B	27.	A
8.	D	18.	A	28.	D
9.	A	19.	B	29.	A
10.	A	20.	D	30.	C

TEST 2

DIRECTIONS: Each question or incomplete statement is followed by several suggested answers or completions. Select the one that BEST answers the question or completes the statement. *PRINT THE LETTER OF THE CORRECT ANSWER IN THE SPACE AT THE RIGHT.*

1. In an AC circuit, a series inductance acting alone causes the current to 1.____
   A. lag the applied voltage by 90 degrees
   B. lead the applied voltage by 90 degrees
   C. lag the applied voltage by 45 degrees
   D. lead the applied voltage by 45 degrees

2. Shock excitation into an L-C circuit is the result of 2.____
   A. a voltage being momentarily introduced
   B. the capacitor may be charged
   C. the inductor may have a voltage induced
   D. all of the above

3. The term cathode ray usually applies to 3.____
   A. a fairly high velocity electron beam
   B. background noise
   C. the logarithm gain of an electron beam
   D. none of the above

4. Shielding an RF inductance 4.____
   A. increases the losses of the inductance
   B. lowers the inductance value and the Q
   C. increases the coil capacity to the shield
   D. all of the above

5. The tendency of a tank circuit to keep oscillating for a time after the excitation energy has been removed is 5.____
   A. push-pull effect   B. flywheel effect
   C. polarizing effect   D. parasitic oscillation

6. Power factor is defined as 6.____
   A. the ratio between the resistance and the impedance in a circuit
   B. the ratio between the true power and the apparent power of a circuit
   C. both A and B
   D. none of the above

7. High or low frequency oscillations occurring in circuits other than the original tank desired output frequencies are 7.____
   A. harmonics   B. parasitic oscillations
   C. hysteresis   D. eddy currents

2 (#2)

8. What are the effects of parasitic oscillations? 8.____
   A. Change of bias
   B. Reduced efficiency of the amplifier tube
   C. Distortion of the modulated wave
   D. All of the above

9. The velocity of propagation of radio frequency waves in free space is 9.____
   A. 300,000 meters/second
   B. 186,284 miles/second
   C. the same as the velocity of light in free space
   D. all of the above

10. To double the resonant frequency of a resonant circuit 10.____
    A. make C one-third of its original value
    B. make L and C both half their original values
    C. decreasing the value of both L and C in any proportion so that their product will be one-half of the original values
    D. none of the above

11. How may the Q of a parallel resonant circuit be increased? 11.____
    A. Increasing coupling to the resonant circuit
    B. Using coil and capacitor supports of special low-loss materials
    C. Both A and B
    D. Decreasing coupling to the resonant circuit

12. If L and C in a parallel resonant circuit resonants at 1000 kHz are so varied that their product remains constant, what will be the resulting resonant frequency? 12.____
    A. 10,000 kHz   B. 100 kHz
    C. 1 MHz   D. None of the above

13. What is the resonant frequency of a tuned circuit consisting of a 500 picofarad capacitor, a 150 microfarad tuning coil, and 10 ohms resistance? 13.____
    A. 581 kHz   B. 753 kHz
    C. 498 kHz   D. None of the above

14. What is voltage regulation as applied to power supplies? 14.____
    A. The ratio of change in voltage between no load and full load to the full-load voltage output
    B. The ratio of output to input voltage
    C. Voltage output of the power supply under full load
    D. The ratio of input to output voltage

15. An EMF may be generated by sound waves by what principle? 15.____
    A. Electrostatic   B. Piezo-electric
    C. Resistance change   D. All of the above

16. How can you correct power factor in an electrical circuit? 16.____
    A. Inductance is used to correct a leading angle.
    B. Capacitance is used to correct a lagging angle.
    C. Neither A nor B
    D. Both A and B

17. Permeability is 17.____
    A. The magnetic field created by a conductor wound on a laminated core and carrying any electric current
    B. The ratio of magnetic flux density in a substance to the magnetizing force which produces it
    C. Polarized molecular alignment in a ferromagnetic material while under the influence of a magnetizing force
    D. Both A and C

18. The time in seconds for a capacitor to attain 63.2% of the applied voltage across its terminals is 18.____
    A. twice the natural period of oscillation of the circuit
    B. varactance
    C. time constant
    D. equal to the ohmic resistance of the circuit

19. What is the reactance of a 2-henry choke at 3000 Hz? 19.____
    A. 5300 ohms   B. 37,680 ohms
    C. 376,800 ohms   D. 53,000 ohms

20. If there is no resistance in either leg of a circuit with an inductance of 5 henrys in parallel with a capacitance of 1 microfarad, what is the equivalent impedance of the parallel network circuit? 20.____
    A. Zero   B. Infinite
    C. Median   D. None of the above

21. What is the total impedance of a series AC circuit having a resistance of 6 ohms, an inductive reactance of 17 ohms, and zero capacitive reactance? 21.____
    A. 15 ohms   B. 27 ohms   C. 18 ohms   D. 5 ohms

22. The total impedance of a series AC circuit with an inductive reactance of 24 ohms, a resistance of 16 ohms, and a capacitive reactance of 16 ohms is 22.____
    A. 2 ohms   B. 16 ohms
    C. 10 ohms   D. none of the above

23. Essentials for making a good solder connection are 23.____
    A. bright, clean parts
    B. plenty of heat with the minimum amount of solder used
    C. discontinue operating on high power
    D. none of the above

24. For protection of personnel handling a transmitter,
    A. ground all exposed metal parts
    B. transmitter is equipped to shunt grounded faults
    C. discontinue operating on high power
    D. none of the above

25. The ratio of peak-to-effective voltage values of a sine wave are
    A. 1.414 to 1
    B. 1 to 0.707
    C. both A and B
    D. neither A nor B

26. The opposition to the creation of magnetic lines of force in a magnetic circuit is known as
    A. reluctance
    B. hysteresis
    C. permeability
    D. eddy currents

27. The ratio of magnetic flux density to the field strength is known as
    A. residual magnetism
    B. permeability
    C. reluctance
    D. none of the above

28. The magnetic force which remains in a substance after the original magnetizing force has been removed is known as
    A. reluctance
    B. residual magnetism
    C. permeability
    D. hysteresis

29. The direction of electron flow through a coil and the manner of winding the turns
    A. influence the direction of magnetic line of force generated by an electromagnet
    B. are determined by the left-hand status rule
    C. are determined by the diameter of the wire and length
    D. both A and C

30. Adding an iron core to an air-core inductance
    A. increases the inductance
    B. decreases the inductance
    C. does not affect the inductance
    D. causes parasitic oscillations in the inductor

KEY (CORRECT ANSWERS)

1.	A	11.	C	21.	C
2.	D	12.	C	22.	B
3.	A	13.	A	23.	D
4.	D	14.	A	24.	A
5.	B	15.	D	25.	C
6.	C	16.	D	26.	A
7.	B	17.	B	27.	B
8.	D	18.	C	28.	B
9.	D	19.	B	29.	A
10.	B	20.	B	30.	A

EXAMINATION SECTION
TEST 1

DIRECTIONS: Each question or incomplete statement is followed by several suggested answers or completions. Select the one that BEST answers the question or completes the statement. *PRINT THE LETTER OF THE CORRECT ANSWER IN THE SPACE AT THE RIGHT.*

1. A copper wire with a resistance of 40 ohms is replaced by a copper wire whose length and diameter are twice that of the original wire.
   The resistance of the new wire is _____ ohms.

   A. 10   B. 20   C. 40   D. 60

2. Three resistors are connected in parallel to a 72-volt battery which supplies them with a total of 6 amperes. The value of a fourth single parallel resistor needed to increase the current drain to 12 amperes is _____ ohms.

   A. 4   B. 6   C. 12   D. 18

3. If an unknown resistor connected across a 60-volt DC source dissipates 100 watts, its resistance is _____ ohms.

   A. 36   B. 48   C. 60   D. 120

4. The MAXIMUM allowable resistance of a resistor that has brown, black, red, and gold color bands is _____ ohms.

   A. 1000   B. 1050   C. 1100   D. 1200

5. If a voltage across a resistor is increased to four times its original value, the power dissipated by the resistor

   A. remains the same
   B. is four times greater
   C. is eight times greater
   D. is sixteen times greater

6.

FIG. 1

For the circuit shown above, the equivalent resistance is _____ ohms.

A. 20.5   B. 50   C. 65   D. 95

7. The material that would BEST shield a permanent magnetic field is

   A. aluminum   B. copper   C. brass   D. iron

8. A material that opposes the flow of magnetic lines of force is said to exhibit

   A. resistivity   B. permeance
   C. reluctance   D. hysteresis

9. The relative ability of a substance to conduct magnetic lines of force, as compared with air, is called

   A. permeability   B. reluctance
   C. retentivity   D. magnetization

10. The combination of current value and turns that makes the STRONGEST electromagnet is _____ turns.

    A. 2000 micro-amperes and 100,000
    B. 6A and 900
    C. 100 mA and 20,000
    D. 4A and 1,200

11. A capacitance of known value connected into a circuit of a known frequency will offer an opposition to the flow of AC based on the relationship

    A. $2\pi fc$
    B. $2\pi fc$ divided by the frequency of the AC
    C. $1/2\pi fc$
    D. wfc

12. In the figure shown at the right, the equivalent inductance is equal to _____ H.

    A. 0.93
    B. 3.83
    C. 4.1
    D. 33.8

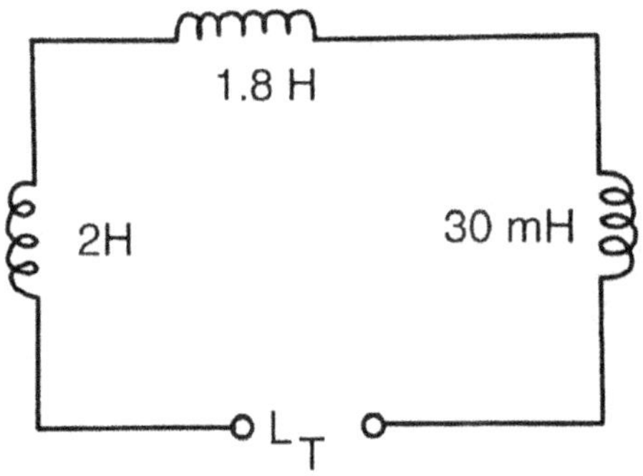

13. In the figure shown at the right, the equivalent inductance L_T equals _____ H.

    A. 5
    B. 6
    C. 12.5
    D. 25

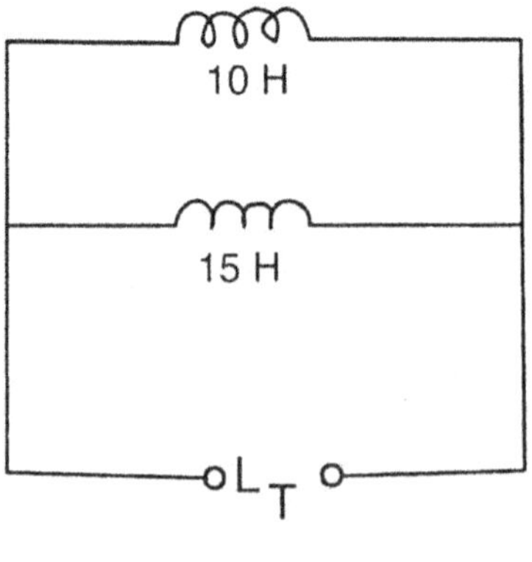

14. In the figure shown at the right, the connections that should be made for MAXIMUM inductance are

    A. A and D, jumper B and C
    B. A and B, jumper A to C and B to D
    C. C and D, jumper A to D and B to C
    D. A and C, jumper B and D

15. Two capacitors rated at 20 microfarads/200 volts each are placed in series. The network is rated at _____ microfarads/ _____ volts.

    A. 40; 200   B. 20; 200   C. 40; 400   D. 10; 400

16. The value of capacitance developed between two metal plates is

    A. proportional to plate area and plate separation
    B. inversely proportional to plate area and plate separation
    C. inversely proportional to plate area and proportional to plate separation
    D. proportional to plate area and inversely proportional to plate separation

17. A 40 microfarad capacitor is connected in series with a parallel combination of a 30 microfarad capacitor and a 60 microfarad capacitor.
    The equivalent capacitance is CLOSEST to _____ uf.

    A. 28   B. 40   C. 60   D. 120

18. The power factor is equal to

    A. one in a reactive circuit and zero in a resistive circuit
    B. zero in a reactive circuit and one in a resistive circuit
    C. a number greater than one in a capacitive circuit
    D. a number greater than one in an inductive circuit

19. If the time required to complete one cycle of AC is 1 millisecond, the frequency per second is _____ Hz.

    A. 10   B. 100   C. 1000   D. 10,000

20. A sine wave voltage of 100 volts rms is applied to a 55-ohm resistor.
    The peak voltage that will appear across the resistor will be CLOSEST to _____ V.

    A. 55   B. 100   C. 141.4   D. 282.8

21. An AC source produces a sinusoidal voltage with a peak-to-peak value of 750 volts.
    The effective value of this voltage is _____ V.

    A. 33   B. 265   C. 375   D. 750

22. The peak value of a sine wave is 150 volts.
    The AVERAGE value taken over a whole cycle is CLOSEST to _____ volts.

    A. zero   B. 75   C. 95.4   D. 150

23. In a circuit that contains only pure capacitance, the current will

    A. lead the voltage by 90°
    B. lag the voltage by 90°
    C. lead the voltage by 180°
    D. be in phase with the voltage

24. An inductor and a lamp are placed in series across an AC supply. As the frequency of the AC supply increases, the lamp

    A. becomes brighter
    B. becomes dimmer
    C. does not change brightness
    D. flashes on and off

25. An RC network has a time constant of 1 second.
    When 100 volts DC is applied to this RC network, the capacitor, after 1 second, will be charged to _____ volts.

    A. 0   B. 37   C. 63   D. 100

KEY (CORRECT ANSWERS)

1.	B	11.	C
2.	C	12.	B
3.	A	13.	B
4.	A	14.	A
5.	D	15.	D
6.	B	16.	D
7.	D	17.	A
8.	C	18.	B
9.	A	19.	C
10.	B	20.	C

21. A
22. C
23. A
24. B
25. C

TEST 2

DIRECTIONS: Each question or incomplete statement is followed by several suggested answers or completions. Select the one that BEST answers the question or completes the statement. *PRINT THE LETTER OF THE CORRECT ANSWER IN THE SPACE AT THE RIGHT.*

1. A resistance in parallel with a tuned circuit will

   A. increase the Q by effectively lowering the series resistance
   B. shift its resonant frequency
   C. lower the Q
   D. decrease the total power dissipated by the entire circuit

   1.____

2. If the tuned circuit used in a radio frequency amplifier has a high Q, it will produce a _____ gain and _____ bandwidth.

   A. high; wide
   B. low; wide
   C. low; narrow
   D. high; narrow

   2.____

Questions 3-5.

DIRECTIONS: Questions 3 through 5 are to be answered on the basis of the following circuit.

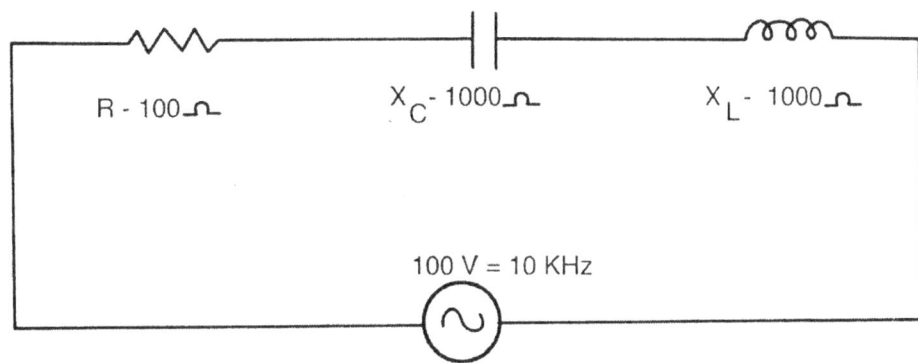

3. The impedance of the above circuit is _____ ohms.

   A. 100   B. 1000   C. 1100   D. 2100

   3.____

4. As the operating frequency of the above generator is increased above resonance, the circuit

   A. impedance decreases
   B. bandwidth increases
   C. current decreases
   D. power factor increases

   4.____

5. If the frequency of the above generator is doubled, the circuit becomes

   A. inductive
   B. capacitive
   C. resistive
   D. an open circuit

   5.____

6.

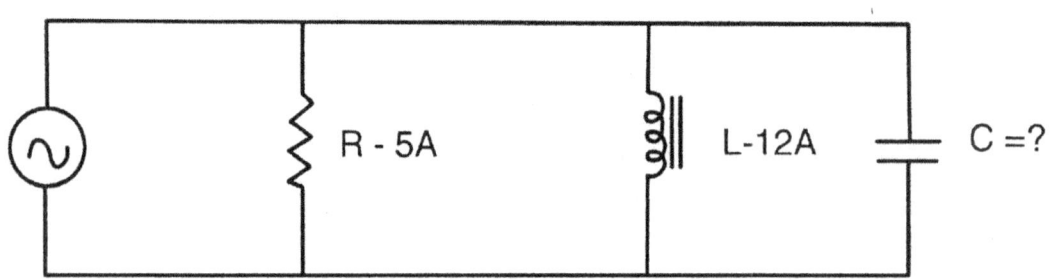

If the parallel circuit shown above is resonant, the current through the capacitive branch is

A. 7A B. 10.9A C. 12A D. 17A

Questions 7-10.

DIRECTIONS: Questions 7 through 10 are to be answered on the basis of the following figures.

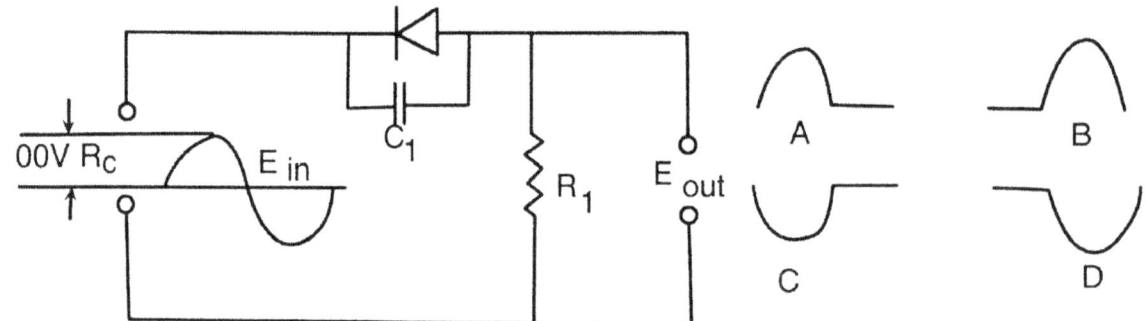

7. The above circuit MOST closely resembles a

   A. half wave voltage doubler supply
   B. full wave transformerless power supply
   C. half wave rectifier circuit
   D. full wave voltage multiplier

8. For the above circuit, the PROPER output waveform is

   A. A B. B C. C D. D

9. For the above circuit, the peak inverse voltage that appears across the diode is

   A. 14.4 volts B. 70.7 volts
   C. 100 volts D. cancelled by Cl

10. The function of Cl in the above circuit is to

    A. protect the diode from voltage transients
    B. protect the diode from current surges
    C. increase the current carrying ability of the diode
    D. increase the PIV rating of the diode

Questions 11-12.

DIRECTIONS: Questions 11 and 12 are to be answered on the basis of the following circuit.

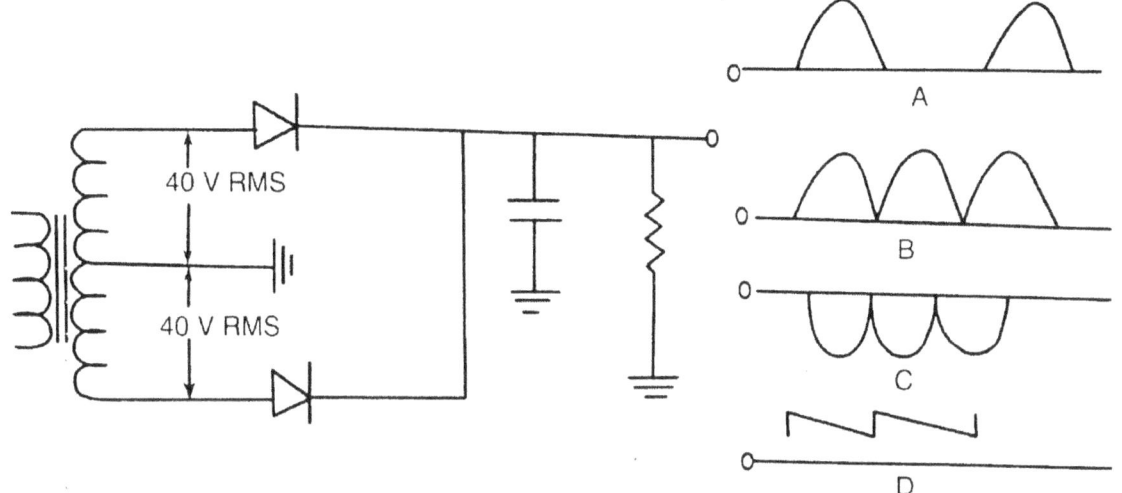

11. The above circuit is BEST described as a

    A. full wave voltage doubler
    B. half wave power supply
    C. full wave rectifier circuit
    D. bridge rectifier

11.____

12. The output waveform for the power supply shown above would MOST closely resemble

    A. A   B. B   C. C   D. D

12.____

13. The type of filter network that provides the BEST overall voltage regulation in a power supply is the

    A. RC filter with resistor input
    B. L type with choke input filter
    C. RC filter with capacitor input
    D. capacitor only filter

13.____

14. A bridge rectifier is operated from a power transformer whose secondary voltage is 40 volts peak-to-peak.
    The peak inverse voltage that will appear across each diode is _____ volts.

    A. 7.07   B. 14.14   C. 20   D. 80

14.____

15. Compared to a bipolar transistor, the field effect transistor

    A. has a high input impedance
    B. is a current operated device
    C. input circuit is normally forward biased
    D. has a high power gain

15.____

Questions 16-17.

DIRECTIONS: Questions 16 and 17 are to be answered on the basis of the following figure.

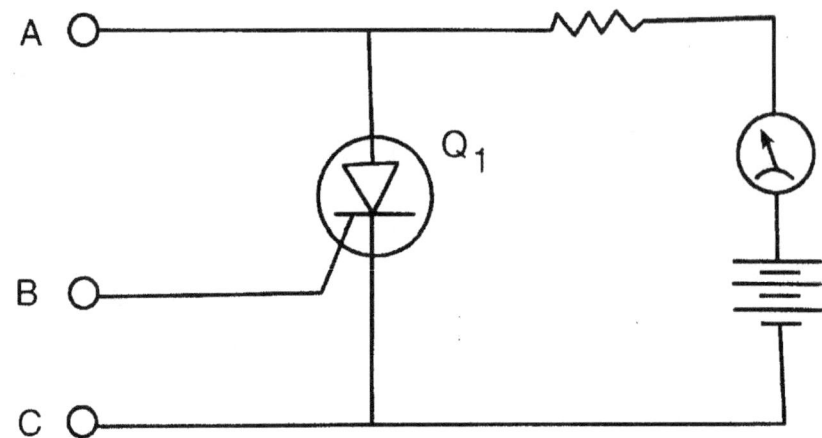

16. In the figure above, when Q_1 is conducting, it is possible to stop conduction by momentarily connecting a jumper wire from

    A. A to B   B. B to C   C. C to A   D. none of the above

17. The above device, Q_1, is a(n)

    A. Diac   B. SCR   C. Triac   D. Varactor

18. When a positive potential is connected to the N region and a negative potential is connected to the P region of a PN junction, it

    A. is forward biased   B. has a low resistance
    C. is effectively shorted   D. exhibits a high resistance

19. A zener diode, when used as a voltage regulator, is

    A. reverse biased at the Zener breakdown point
    B. forward biased at the Zener point
    C. set up so that it has no bias voltage
    D. adjusted for any voltage output

20. A varactor diode

    A. increases its capacitance when its reverse bias is decreased
    B. decreases its capacitance when its reverse bias is decreased
    C. has a fixed capacitance
    D. none of the above

21. An NPN transistor is forward biased when

    A. the base is made positive with respect to the emitter
    B. the base is made negative with respect to the emitter
    C. its collector current is at minimum
    D. the collector is made positive with respect to the emitter

22. When used as a Class A amplifier, a bipolar transistor is set up with its base 22._____

    A. reverse biased and its collector forward biased
    B. forward biased and its collector reverse biased
    C. and collector forward biased
    D. and collector reverse biased

23. Base current in an operating NPN transistor is 23._____

    A. small compared to the emitter current
    B. large compared to the emitter current
    C. equal to the emitter current
    D. non-existent

24. The vacuum tube parameter that describes the effect of control grid voltage on plate current is called the 24._____

    A. dynamic plate resistance
    B. amplification factor
    C. transconductance
    D. input impedance

25. The PRIMARY function of a suppressor grid in a pentode vacuum tube is to reduce 25._____

    A. harmonic distortion
    B. plate resistance
    C. the effects of secondary emission
    D. interelectrode capacitance from control grid to cathode

KEY (CORRECT ANSWERS)

1.	C	11.	C
2.	D	12.	B
3.	A	13.	B
4.	C	14.	B
5.	A	15.	A
6.	C	16.	C
7.	C	17.	B
8.	D	18.	D
9.	B	19.	A
10.	B	20.	B

21. A
22. B
23. A
24. C
25. C

TEST 3

DIRECTIONS: Each question or incomplete statement is followed by several suggested answers or completions. Select the one that BEST answers the question or completes the statement. *PRINT THE LETTER OF THE CORRECT ANSWER IN THE SPACE AT THE RIGHT.*

1. In a tetrode or pentode vacuum tube, the plate current will increase when the   1.____

    A. control grid voltage is made more negative with respect to the cathode
    B. control grid voltage is made more positive with respect to the cathode
    C. plate voltage is decreased
    D. screen grid voltage is made less positive

2. In a pentode vacuum tube, the cathode current is 10 mA and the plate current 7 mA. The screen grid current is _____ mA.   2.____

    A. 3   B. 7   C. 10   D. 17

Questions 3-5.

DIRECTIONS: Questions 3 through 5 are to be answered on the basis of the following circuit.

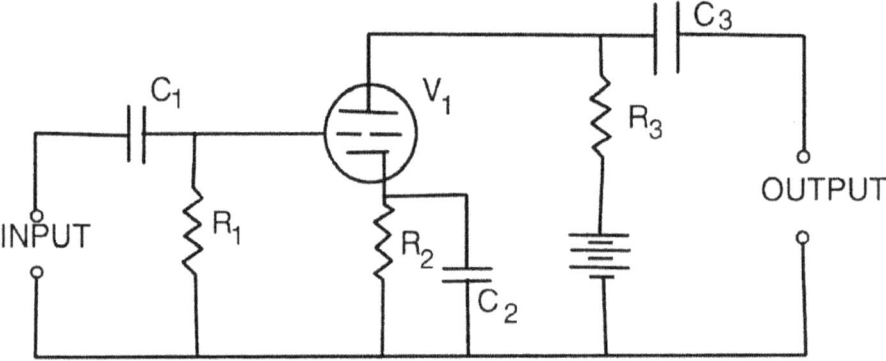

3. The low frequency response for the above circuit can be improved by   3.____

    A. decreasing the value of C_1
    B. increasing the value of C_2
    C. reducing the value of R_1
    D. decreasing the value of C_3

4. The triode voltage amplifier shown above has equal plate resistance and load resistance. If the amplification factor is 40, the stage gain is   4.____

    A. 10   B. 15   C. 20   D. 40

5. Removal of C_2 from the above circuit will   5.____

    A. increase the gain of the stage
    B. lower the gain of the stage
    C. decrease the bandwidth of the stage
    D. increase the distortion level

Questions 6-9.

DIRECTIONS: Questions 6 through 9 are to be answered on the basis of the following circuit.

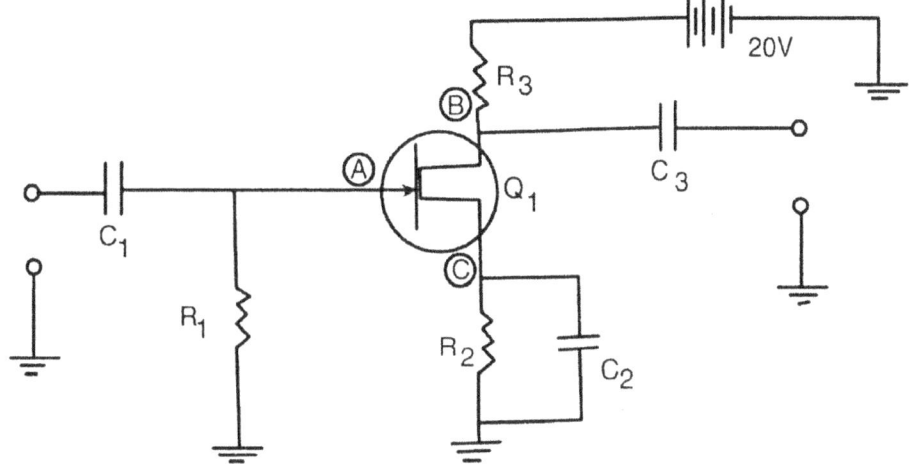

6. In the above circuit, the terminals of Q_1 correspond to A = _____, B = _____, C = _____.

   A. gate; source; drain
   B. grid; drain; source
   C. gate; drain; source
   D. drain; gate; source

   6._____

7. In the above circuit, the active device is a

   A. Mosfet
   B. Jfet
   C. Triac
   D. Bipolar transistor

   7._____

8. In the above amplifier circuit, the output signal when compared to the input signal, will be

   A. 180° out of phase because this is a common drain circuit
   B. 180° out of phase because this is a common source circuit
   C. in phase because this is a common gate circuit
   D. in phase because this is a common collector circuit

   8._____

9. In the above circuit, neglecting the small voltage drop across R_2, the theoretical maximum peak-to-peak output signal will be _____ volts.

   A. 5 B. 7.5 C. 10 D. 20

   9._____

10. An amplifier circuit that allows output current to flow for only 180° of the input cycle is defined as

    A. Class A
    B. Class B
    C. Class AB
    D. defective

    10._____

11. An amplifier circuit that allows output current to flow for 360° of the input cycle is defined as Class

    A. A B. AB C. B D. C

    11._____

12. Two voltage amplifiers are connected in cascade. The gain of the first stage is 15, and the gain of the second stage is 20.
    The overall gain will be

    A. 35   B. 300   C. 335   D. 350

Questions 13-15.

DIRECTIONS: Questions 13 through 15 are to be answered on the basis of the following circuit.

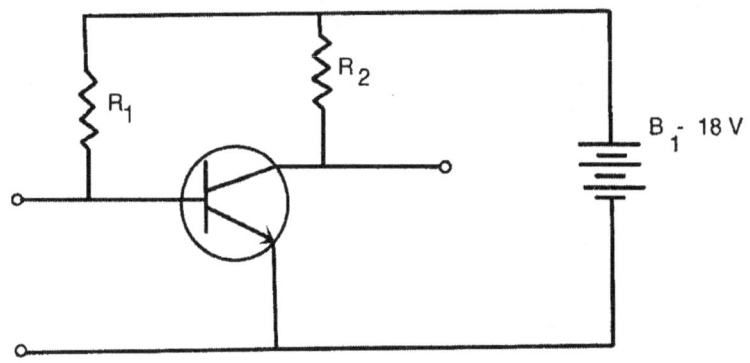

13. The above circuit is a common _____ configuration.

    A. base   B. emitter   C. collector   D. source

14. Calculate the value of R_1 necessary for the above circuit, given a required base current of 30 microamperes.

    A. 20K   B. 200K   C. 400K   D. 600K

15. The addition of a resistor in the emitter lead of the circuit shown above would tend to

    A. increase the distortion generated in the stage
    B. increase the stage gain
    C. increase clipping
    D. reduce thermal runaway

16.

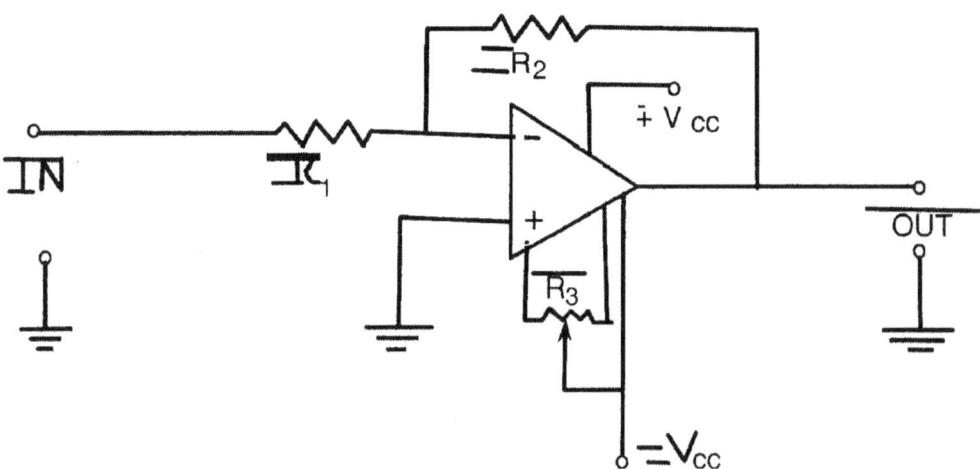

The function of R_3 in the above circuit is to

A. adjust the gain of the amplifier
B. set frequency compensation
C. balance out any offset voltage (offset null)
D. act as the volume control

17. A triode amplifier stage uses a tube that has a plate resistance of 5000 ohms. The GREATEST voltage gain will be obtained with a plate load resistance value of _____ ohms.

    A. 1000   B. 2,500   C. 5,000   D. 10,000

18. The semiconductor device that can be destroyed by electrostatic shock due to handling is the

    A. MOSFET   B. JFET
    C. TRIAC   D. Bipolar Transistor

19. A transistor audio power amplifier that employs a pair of complementary output transistors will normally NOT contain

    A. heat sinks   B. capacitors
    C. resistors   D. output transformers

20. A problem unique to transistorized push-pull Class B audio power amplifiers is

    A. even harmonic distortion
    B. overdrive
    C. crossover distortion
    D. thermal runaway

21. A junction transistor connected as a common collector amplifier has a

    A. high voltage gain
    B. low input impedance and low output impedance
    C. high input and high output impedance
    D. high input and low output impedance

22. The current gain of a junction transistor operated as a common base amplifier is ALWAYS

    A. slightly less than one
    B. exactly one
    C. slightly greater than one
    D. much greater than one

23. The transistor connected as a common emitter amplifier can provide

    A. both a voltage and current gain
    B. only voltage gain
    C. only current gain
    D. a minimum power gain

24. The use of negative feedback in an amplifier stage causes 24.____

    A. decreased bandwidth
    B. reduced gain
    C. instability at the high frequency end of the response
    D. oscillation

25. To convert a 0-1 mA meter to a 0-1 voltmeter, we must add a resistance of _____ with   25.____
    the meter.

    A. 10 ohms in parallel   B. 10 ohms in series
    C. 1K or more in parallel   D. 1K or more in series

KEY (CORRECT ANSWERS)

1. B   11. A
2. A   12. B
3. B   13. B
4. C   14. D
5. C   15. D

6. C   16. C
7. B   17. C
8. B   18. A
9. B   19. D
10. B   20. C

21. B
22. A
23. A
24. B
25. D

TEST 4

DIRECTIONS: Each question or incomplete statement is followed by several suggested answers or completions. Select the one that BEST answers the question or completes the statement. *PRINT THE LETTER OF THE CORRECT ANSWER IN THE SPACE AT THE RIGHT.*

1. When taking voltage measurements in a high resistance circuit, the BEST instrument to use for maximum accuracy is the   1._____

    A. one thousand ohms per volt voltmeter
    B. twenty thousand ohms per volt voltmeter
    C. field effect transistor voltmeter (FETVOM)
    D. iron vane type voltmeter

2. A 0-1 mA 50 ohm meter must have its range increased to 0-100 mA. In order to do this, we must wire a _____ value resistance in _____ with the meter _____.   2._____

    A. high; parallel; (1/2 M)
    B. low; parallel; (0.5 ohms)
    C. high; series; (1/2 M)
    D. low; series; (0.5 ohms)

Questions 3-5.

DIRECTIONS: Questions 3 through 5 are to be answered on the basis of the following figures.

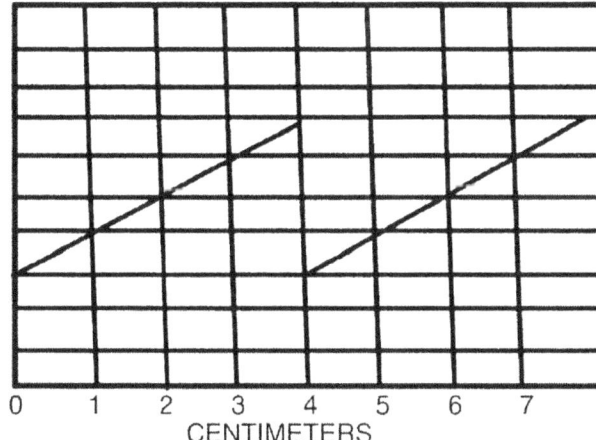 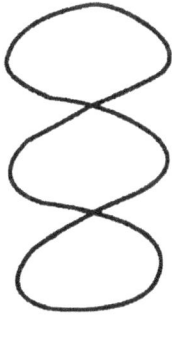

3. The waveshape shown above is observed on an oscilloscope whose vertical multiplier control is set at X10. Each vertical division is calibrated for IV pp on the XI setting. The peak-to-peak voltage of the waveform is   3._____

    A. 6V
    B. 60V
    C. 600V
    D. insufficient data to compute answer

45

4. A sine wave whose frequency is unknown is applied to the vertical input of an oscilloscope. A 600 Hz sine wave is applied to the horizontal input. The Lissajou pattern shown above is displayed on the screen.
   The unknown frequency is

   A. 200 Hz   B. 600 Hz   C. 1.2 KHz   D. 1.8 KHz

5. The waveform shown above is observed on an oscilloscope screen whose time base is set at 0.1 milliseconds per centimeter.
   The APPROXIMATE frequency of the waveform is _____ Hz.

   A. 1,250   B. 2,000   C. 2,500   D. 5,000

Questions 6-9.

DIRECTIONS: Questions 6 through 9 are to be answered on the basis of the following circuit.

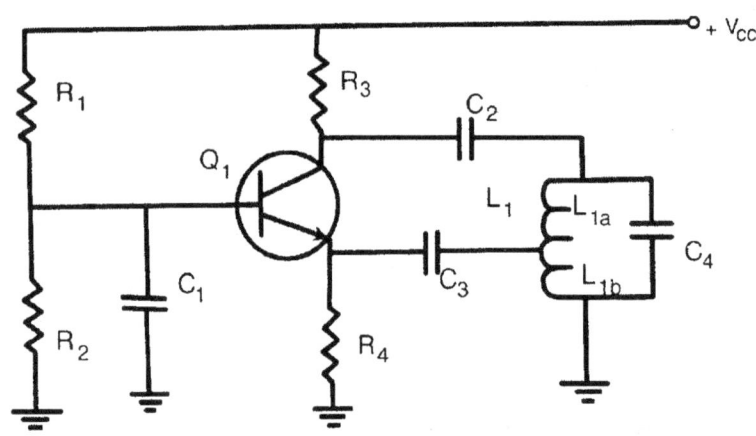

6. The amount of feedback in the circuit shown above is determined by the ratio of

   A. R_1 to R_2 B. R_3 to R_4 C. C_2 to C_3 D. L_{1a} to L_{1b}

7. The coupling and feedback capacitors (C_2, C_3) shown above

   A. determine the frequency of oscillation with L_1
   B. block AC from the bias network
   C. provide the 180° phase shift (90° each)
   D. isolate the tank circuit from DC

8. The frequency of oscillation in the above circuit is determined by the

   A. RC values   B. LC tank circuit
   C. feedback level   D. C_1, R_2

9. The circuit shown above is a(n)

   A. Hartley oscillator, series fed
   B. Hartley oscillator, shunt fed
   C. Colpitts oscillator
   D. Armstrong oscillator

10. A three-input NAND gate may be used as an inverter by

    A. paralleling the three inputs
    B. paralleling the three inputs and grounding the output
    C. feeding one input and grounding the other two
    D. grounding all three inputs

11. To produce a logical one-output from a three input NAND gate, the inputs must be

    A. all placed at logical one
    B. set for two at zero and one at logical one
    C. set for one at zero and two at logical one
    D. all placed at logical zero

12. The AVC circuit of a superheterodyne receiver

    A. prevents overload on weak signals when the AGC control voltage is usually lowest
    B. derives its control voltage from the first detector
    C. adjusts the receiver gain for different signal strengths
    D. reduces the level of noise between stations

Questions 13-15.

DIRECTIONS: Questions 13 through 15 are to be answered on the basis of the following circuit.

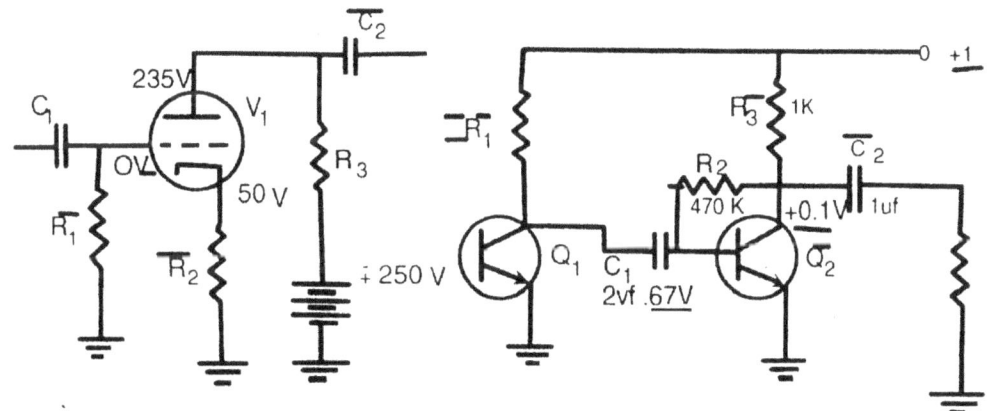

13. When the above circuit is operating properly, the normal tube element voltages measured to ground will read (disregard element voltages shown)

    A. G) 0V, P) 150V, K) 3V
    B. G) 0V, P) 200V, K) 50V
    C. G) -3V, P) 200V, K) 3V
    D. G) 3V, P) 150V, K) -3V

14. The above circuit is inoperative.
    According to the voltage measurements shown, the MOST likely fault is

    A. R_1 open
    B. R_2 open
    C. R_3 shorted or dropped in value
    D. V_1 defective

15. The above circuit is not working properly. According to the voltage measurements shown, the MOST likely fault is

   A. R_2 reduced in value
   B. R_3 open
   C. C_1 leaky
   D. C_2 shorted

16. When the IF amplifier of a receiver is tuned to 456 KHz and the receiver is tuned to receive a 1200 KHz signal, the image interference signal will be at _____ KHz.

   A. 456 B. 1200 C. 1656 D. 2112

17. The GREATEST degree of selectivity of an AM or FM superheterodyne receiver is determined by the characteristics of the _____ stage(s).

   A. RF B. AF C. IF D. mixer

18. In an AM superheterodyne receiver, most of the signal amplification occurs in the _____ stage(s).

   A. RF B. mixer C. IF D. AF

19. A variable capacitor in a radio receiver has a non-linear capacitance curve when rotated. The reason for this is to

   A. provide fine tuning
   B. enable the band to be spread out as much as possible
   C. provide linear frequency calibration on the dial
   D. provide a stable oscillator signal

Questions 20-23.

DIRECTIONS: Questions 20 through 23 are to be answered on the basis of the following figure.

20. The gate that produces a logical one output only when both inputs are a logical one is called a(n) _____ gate and is shown in _____ above.

   A. NAND; D B. NOR; B C. AND; B D. OR; E

21. The gate that produces a logical one output when one or both inputs are a logical one is called a(n) _____ gate and is shown in _____ above.

   A. AND; B B. OR; C C. AND; D D. OR; B

22. Symbol A above represents a(n)

   A. inverter
   B. OR gate
   C. AND gate
   D. NOR gate

23. The above symbol used to represent an exclusive OR gate is   23.____

   A. C   B. D   C. E   D. F

24. A mixer stage of a superheterodyne has an input signal of 1455 KHz from the local oscil-   24.____
   lator and a 1000 KHz carrier signal from the RF stage.
   The mixer output current contains the following frequencies:

   A. 455 KHz, 910 KHz
   B. 1455 KHz, 1000 KHz
   C. 1455 KHz, 1000 KHz, 455 KHz
   D. 1455 KHz, 1000 KHz, 455 KHz, 2455 KHz

25. The loudness control in a high fidelity amplifier serves   25.____

   A. the same purpose as a conventional level control
   B. to compensate by boosting the high and low ends at low volume levels
   C. to boost the high and low ends at high volume levels
   D. to boost the low end and drop the high end at low volume levels

---

KEY (CORRECT ANSWERS)

1.	B	11.	D
2.	B	12.	C
3.	B	13.	B
4.	D	14.	A
5.	C	15.	A
6.	D	16.	C
7.	D	17.	A
8.	B	18.	C
9.	B	19.	A
10.	A	20.	C

21. B
22. A
23. D
24. D
25. D

TEST 5

DIRECTIONS: Each question or incomplete statement is followed by several suggested answers or completions. Select the one that BEST answers the question or completes the statement. *PRINT THE LETTER OF THE CORRECT ANSWER IN THE SPACE AT THE RIGHT.*

1. The impedance of a speaker

    A. is rated at approximately 4000 Hz
    B. varies with frequency
    C. is lowest at resonance
    D. remains fixed at all operating frequencies

1._____

Questions 2-3.

DIRECTIONS: Questions 2 and 3 are to be answered on the basis of the following circuit.

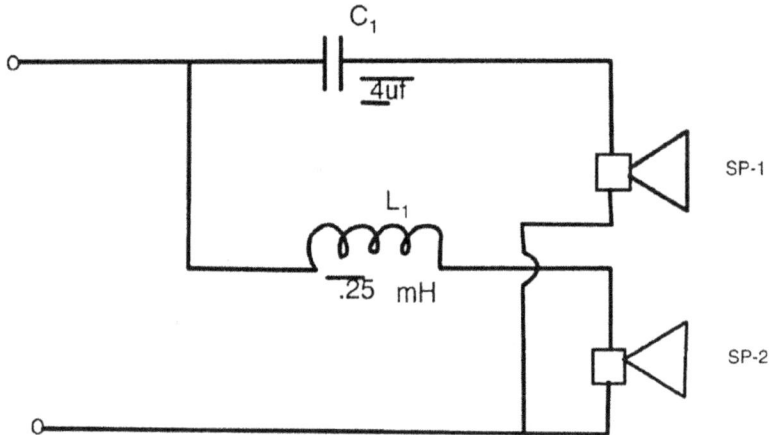

2. In the above circuit,

    A. SP1 is a woofer and SP2 is the midrange
    B. SP1 is the woofer and SP2 is the tweeter
    C. SP1 is the tweeter and SP2 is the woofer
    D. SP1 is the woofer and SP2 is an electrostatic tweeter

2._____

3. The function of the $L_1 C_1$ network above is to

    A. suppress transients before they reach SP1
    B. cut off the low and high ends of the audio spectrum to prevent overload
    C. keep the low frequencies from SP1 and block the high frequencies from SP2
    D. keep the low frequencies from SP2 and block the high frequencies from SP1

3._____

4. When the left and right channel speakers are improperly phased in a stereo system,

    A. there is a marked drop in volume
    B. the high frequency response drops off
    C. the low frequency response drops off
    D. there is no audible effect

4._____

5. A flashlight contains four batteries connected in series. If each battery delivers 1.5 volts, the voltage delivered to the bulb if one battery is installed backwards is _____ V.   5.____

   A. 3.0   B. 4.5   C. 6.0   D. 7.5

6. The function of an RF amplifier in a superheterodyne receiver is to   6.____

   A. provide the gain that determines receiver sensitivity
   B. provide the tuned circuits to determine receiver selectivity
   C. increase the receiver's ability to produce cross-modulation
   D. aid in the rejection of image interference

7. A choke input filter is sometimes preferred over a capacitor input filter in a power supply because it   7.____

   A. has better regulation
   B. will produce a higher output voltage
   C. will produce a lower output voltage
   D. will increase the current flow

8. The purpose of a line by-pass capacitor is to   8.____

   A. reduce hum/noise   B. increase the line voltage
   C. regulate line voltage   D. reduce oscillation

9. The term *carrier* means the _____ radio wave.   9.____

   A. amplitude of a   B. demodulated
   C. frequency of the   D. unmodulated

10. Inductance is that property of an inductor which   10.____

    A. aids the flow of current
    B. causes the circuit to act as a pure resistance
    C. opposes any change in current flow
    D. increases the voltage

11. The term *directivity* in a receiving antenna array refers to the   11.____

    A. sharpness of signal concentration in a given direction
    B. direction in which radiation is suppressed
    C. number of side lobes that appear
    D. driven element

12. The SIMPLEST test for determining whether or not a vacuum tube oscillator is functioning is a measurement of its   12.____

    A. plate potential   B. grid-bias potential
    C. cathode potential   D. frequency

13. When voltage is measured with a VTVM, the reading will usually be higher than that obtained with a 1000 ohm per volt multimeter because the   13.____

    A. VTVM has a larger dial scale
    B. VTVM draws little current
    C. VTVM is less accurate
    D. VOM has less resistance

14. Peaking coils are used in video amplifiers to improve

    A. low frequency response
    B. response to mid frequency signals
    C. the response to high frequencies
    D. the response to color burst

15. The impedance at the center of a folded dipole FM antenna is _____ ohms.

    A. 52   B. 72   C. 150   D. 300

16. Multiple speakers are properly phased when the voice coils

    A. move in opposite directions as in push-pull
    B. are wound in the same direction
    C. are wired in series
    D. move in the same direction together

17. The signal that is fed directly into the speaker voice coil is

    A. a sound wave   B. AF current
    C. pulsating DC   D. rectified AF

18. Negative feedback is used in amplifiers to

    A. increase gain
    B. eliminate degeneration
    C. reduce interelectrode capacitance
    D. reduce distortion

19. If the center tap of a full-wave rectifier transformer should open, the DC output voltage of the power supply would be

    A. doubled
    B. reduced to approximately half
    C. unchanged
    D. zero

20. A resistance check of a solid state rectifier in good condition should show

    A. the same resistance in either direction
    B. a high resistance in one direction and a low resistance in the other
    C. a low resistance in both directions
    D. a high resistance in both directions

21. A bridge type rectifier

    A. uses a center tapped transformer
    B. has a full-wave output
    C. has a half-wave output

Questions 22-24.

DIRECTIONS: Questions 22 through 24 are to be answered on the basis of the following figure.

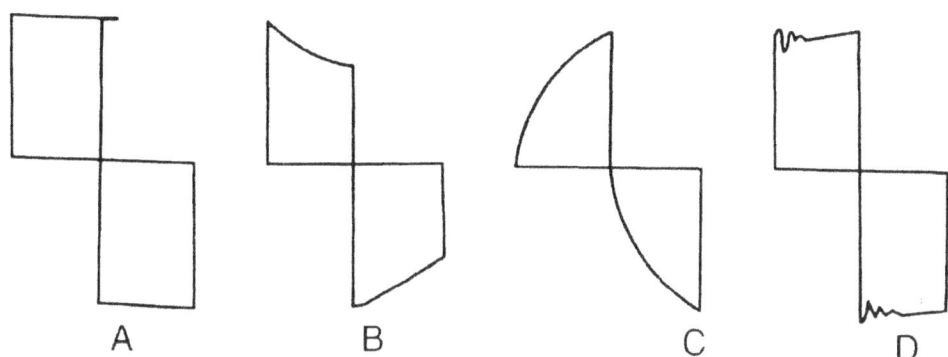

22. The input to a video amplifier is a perfect 500 Hz. square wave. If the low frequency response is poor, the output waveform shown above will be CLOSEST to

    A. A   B. B   C. C   D. D

23. The input to a video amplifier is a perfect 30 KHz square wave. If the high frequency response is poor, the output waveform shown above will be CLOSEST to

    A. A   B. B   C. C   D. D

24. The input to a video amplifier is a perfect square wave at 30 KHz and the output waveform appears above in D. The PROBABLE cause will be

    A. lagging phase shift at the high frequency end of the response
    B. poor high frequency response
    C. insufficient mid-frequency response (damping)
    D. excessive high frequency response (ringing)

25. The taper used for an audio level control is

    A. linear   B. logarithmic
    C. reverse   D. sinusoidal

KEY (CORRECT ANSWERS)

1. B
2. C
3. C
4. D
5. B

6. B
7. A
8. A
9. D
10. C

11. A
12. D
13. B
14. C
15. D

16. D
17. B
18. D
19. A
20. B

21. B
22. B
23. C
24. D
25. B

EXAMINATION SECTION
TEST 1

DIRECTIONS: Each question or incomplete statement is followed by several suggested answers or completions. Select the one that BEST answers the question or completes the statement. *PRINT THE LETTER OF THE CORRECT ANSWER IN THE SPACE AT THE RIGHT.*

1. Three resistors, each of 12 ohms, connected in parallel with each other, are connected in series to a resistor of 6 ohms and to a 60 volt source.
   The current, in amperes, through the 6 ohms resistor will be

   A. 5   B. 6   C. 10   D. 15

   1.____

2. Two electrical condensers have capacitances of 9 and 18 microfarads, respectively, are connected in series.
   The capacitance, in microfarads, of the two connected together will be

   A. 6   B. 9   C. 13.5   D. 27

   2.____

3. The current in a coil having an inductance of 32 millihenries increases in magnitude from 2 to 6 amperes in 0.05 second.
   The voltage of self-induction will equal

   A. 1.28   B. 1.60   C. 1.92   D. 2.56

   3.____

4. A variable electrical condenser of the type used in radio sets is completely immersed in oil whose dielectric strength is 3.5.
   As compared to its former state, its

   A. ability to withstand high voltages has been reduced
   B. capacitance has been increased
   C. capacitance has been decreased
   D. capacitance remains unaffected

   4.____

5. A shunt motor having an armature whose resistance is 0.5 ohm is attached to a 120 volt supply. The armature current at full speed is 10 amperes.
   The back EMF, in volts, will be

   A. 5   B. 10   C. 115   D. 125

   5.____

6. An electron stream sent horizontally through a magnetic field whose lines of force are horizontal and at right angles to the electron stream will

   A. curve in a horizontal plane
   B. curve in a vertical plane
   C. curve in a plane neither horizontal nor vertical
   D. pass through without curving

   6.____

7. In a series wound DC electrical generator, the current in the line is

   A. the same as the field current
   B. half the current through either brush
   C. twice the current through either brush
   D. independent of the field current

   7.____

55

8. The MOST economical 0.1 mfd condenser to be used, without danger of shorting, on a 250-volt AC line is one whose DC working voltage is rated at

   A. 250 B. 300 C. 400 D. 600

9. As the frequency of an alternating EMF in a given circuit increases, the current in the circuit at first increases, then decreases.
   The circuit contains

   A. only capacitative reactance
   B. only inductive reactance
   C. both capacitative and inductive reactance
   D. a constant impedance

10. A storage cell is connected in series with a resistance of 0.3 ohms.
    If the resistance of the cell is 0.2 ohms and its EMF is 2.5 volts, the current, expressed in amperes, in the circuit is

    A. 1/5 B. 5 C. 7.5 D. 12.5

11. A battery has an open circuit voltage of 20 volts and an internal resistance of 0.25 ohm. When it delivers a current of 10 amperes, the terminal voltage will be

    A. 15 B. 17.5 C. 18 D. 20

12. The core of an electromagnet is made of soft iron because soft iron

    A. is an electrical conductor
    B. is easily magnetized and demagnetized
    C. is easy to shape
    D. retains its magnetism

13. The wire in the primary of a step-up transformer is usually thicker than the wire in the secondary because the primary has the

    A. higher current   B. higher resistance
    C. higher voltage   D. lower current

14. Direct current is necessary in order to

    A. charge storage batteries
    B. operate lights
    C. produce heat
    D. run electric motors

15. Very small electric currents are measured by a(n)

    A. galvanometer   B. micrometer
    C. ohmmeter   D. wattmeter

16. Of the following, the STRONGEST electromagnet is one having _____ amperes and _____ turns.

    A. 5; 10 B. 10; 5 C. 5; 5 D. 10; 10

17. In describing an alternating current, the term *60 cycles per second* refers to the

    A. amplitude B. frequency C. voltage D. wavelength

18. In a parallel circuit, the device with the LOWEST resistance has the

   A. least heating effect   B. highest wattage
   C. lowest current   D. lowest voltage drop

19. When a current is made to flow in a circuit consisting of two unlike metals, heat is absorbed at one of the junctions and given off at the other junction.
   This phenomenon is known as the _____ effect

   A. Tyndall   B. Stark   C. Purkinje   D. Peltier

20. Assume that a length of wire having a resistance of 20 ohms is cut into four equal lengths. The four resistors then are connected in parallel with each other and their resistance measured.
   The resistance, in ohms, will be

   A. 1.25   B. 2.50   C. 5   D. 10

21. Two adjacent turns in a helical coil through which a constant current is passing will

   A. repel each other
   B. attract each other
   C. have no effect on each other
   D. have a voltage induced in them

22. When several capacitors are connected in series and to a source of direct current, each capacitor must have the same

   A. voltage   B. dielectric strength
   C. charge   D. capacitance

23. The current in an alternating current circuit is equal to the voltage multiplied by the

   A. impedance   B. admittance
   C. capacitance   D. inductance

24. The penetrating power of the x-rays produced by a Coolidge x-ray tube can be increased by increasing the

   A. number of electrons emitted from the filament
   B. distance between cathode and anode
   C. mass of the anode
   D. voltage between cathode and anode

25. The combined resistance, in ohms, of four 100-ohm resistors connected in series is

   A. 100   B. 200   C. 25   D. 400

26. Four resistors of sixty ohms each are connected in parallel.
   Their combined resistance, in ohms, is

   A. 15   B. 30   C. 60   D. 240

27. Resistors of 5, 10, 15, and 30 ohms are connected in series to a battery.
   The GREATEST voltage drop will be across the resistor of _____ ohms.

   A. 5   B. 10   C. 15   D. 30

28. Eight Christmas tree lamps are connected in series on a 120-volt circuit. The voltage across each lamp is

   A. 15   B. 112   C. 120   D. 960

29. A flow of electricity in a copper wire consists of a movement of

   A. ions   B. electrons   C. positrons   D. protons

30. A wire 50 feet long has a resistance of 10 ohms. The resistance of 25 feet of this wire is _____ ohms.

   A. 2.5   B. 5   C. 20   D. 40

31. All of the following devices can be operated from a steady direct current EXCEPT a

   A. flatiron
   B. rheostat
   C. toaster
   D. transformer

32. The alloy used for lead-in wires of electric lamps is chosen PRINCIPALLY because it

   A. does not expand on heating
   B. expands at the same rate as glass
   C. has a high specific heat
   D. has a low melting point

33. A voltmeter is a galvanometer that has its movable coil connected with a _____ resistance in _____.

   A. high; parallel
   B. high; series
   C. low; parallel
   D. low; series

34. A commutator on a direct-current motor

   A. reverses the direction of the current in the field magnet
   B. reverses the direction of the current in the armature coils
   C. changes low voltage DC to higher voltage DC
   D. changes low voltage AC to higher voltage AC

35. One great advantage of AC over DC is that AC

   A. can be stored
   B. can be transmitted more economically
   C. operates heating devices better
   D. requires less insulation

36. Steady direct current cannot be used to operate a(n)

   A. doorbell
   B. electric heater
   C. lamp
   D. transformer

37. Only direct-current electricity may be used to

   A. operate a transformer
   B. charge a storage battery
   C. heat a radio-tube filament
   D. operate a doorbell

5 (#1)

38. In speaking of 60-cycle alternating current, the term *60 cycle* refers to   38.____

   A. amplitude   B. frequency
   C. velocity   D. wavelength

39. Of the following, the device that should NOT be connected to a DC source is a   39.____

   A. flatiron   B. heating coil
   C. lamp   D. transformer

40. The armature in an electric doorbell moves away from the magnet because it is   40.____

   A. moved back by the electromagnet
   B. moved back by the spring
   C. repelled by the gong
   D. repelled by the interrupter

41. A condenser is used to   41.____

   A. change AC to DC   B. charge batteries
   C. generate electricity D. store electricity

42. The potential difference in a circuit is measured in   42.____

   A. amperes   B. ohms   C. volts   D. watts

43. The current in a fuse is _____ the current in the circuit it protects.   43.____

   A. much less than   B. the same as
   C. slightly greater than D. much greater than

44. A condenser is connected in series with a 25-watt lamp to a 120-volt DC source.   44.____
    The lamp will

   A. operate normally   B. burn out
   C. glow dimly   D. not operate

45. A galvanometer has a resistance of 50 ohms and requires 0.05 amperes for full-scale   45.____
    The voltage required for half-scale deflection is

   A. 0.0001   B. 0.05   C. 1.25   D. 2.5

46. If the capacitance in an oscillator circuit of frequency F is increased fourfold, the frequency of the oscillator becomes   46.____

   A. F/4   B. F/2   C. 2F   D. 4F

47. In circuit A, one ampere of AC flows for 1 hour and generates X calories. In circuit B, one   47.____
    ampere of DC flows for 1 hour.
    The heat generated in circuit B is

   A. 0.707X   B. the same as in A
   C. $\dfrac{X}{0.707}$ D. 0.24 IRT

48. Two 50-watt, 120-volt heaters are connected in parallel to a 120-volt DC line. The power consumption is now X times as great as it would be if they were connected in series. Assuming no change in resistance, X will be

    A. 2 B. 1/2 C. 1/4 D. 4

49. In an AC circuit in which the current and voltage are out of phase by 90°, an ammeter reads 2 and a voltmeter reads 120.
    The power expended by this circuit, in watts, equals

    A. zero B. 60 C. 120 D. 240

50. A voltmeter showed a reading, when connected to a circuit carrying a sinusoidal alternating current, of 100 volts (RMS value).
    The MAXIMUM instantaneous voltage was

    A. 100 B. 141 C. 173 D. 200

KEY (CORRECT ANSWERS)

1. B	11. B	21. B	31. D	41. D
2. A	12. B	22. C	32. B	42. C
3. D	13. A	23. B	33. B	43. B
4. B	14. A	24. D	34. B	44. D
5. C	15. A	25. D	35. B	45. C
6. B	16. D	26. A	36. D	46. B
7. A	17. B	27. D	37. B	47. B
8. C	18. B	28. A	38. B	48. D
9. C	19. D	29. B	39. D	49. A
10. B	20. A	30. B	40. B	50. B

TEST 2

DIRECTIONS: Each question or incomplete statement is followed by several suggested answers or completions. Select the one that BEST answers the question or completes the statement. *PRINT THE LETTER OF THE CORRECT ANSWER IN THE SPACE AT THE RIGHT.*

1. A three-element vacuum tube in an electric circuit

    A. generates signals of increased voltage
    B. amplifies the grid bias
    C. controls the electron flow in the circuit
    D. rectifies the B-battery output
    E. increases the signal frequency

    1._____

2. A simple series circuit consists of a cell, an ammeter, and a rheostat of resistance R. The ammeter reads 5 amps. When the resistance of the rheostat is increased by 2 ohms, the ammeter reading drops to 4 amps.
    The original resistance, in ohms, of the rheostat R is

    A. 2.5 B. 4.0 C. 8.0 D. 10.0 E. 12.0

    2._____

3. Two lamps need 50V and 2 amp each in order to operate at a desired brilliancy. If they are to be connected in series across a 120V line, the resistance, in ohms, of the rheostat that must be placed in series with the lamps needs to be

    A. 4 B. 10 C. 20 D. 100 E. 200

    3._____

4. As the photon is a quantum in electromagnetic field theory, which one of the following is considered to be the quantum in the nuclear field?

    A. Neutrino   B. Electron   C. Meson
    D. Neutron   E. None of the above

    4._____

5. Which symbol represents an electrical ground connection?

    5._____

6. Which of the following circuits could you wire from the diagram at the right?
    A. Code oscillator
    B. Doorbell system
    C. Electric chime
    D. Radio receiving set
    E. Electric train signal

    6._____

7. The rate of electron flow in an electric circuit is measured with a(n)

    A. ammeter   B. voltmeter   C. ohmmeter
    D. wattmeter   E. none of the above

    7._____

61

8. Which one of the following is characteristic of a parallel electrical circuit?

   A. The current is the same in all parts of the circuit.
   B. The voltage across all the branches is the same.
   C. A break through any part of the circuit will stop the flow of current throughout the circuit.
   D. The total resistance is equal to the sum of the resistances of the component parts.

9. When sphere A, with a large negative charge, is touched by sphere B, with a smaller negative charge, which one of the following will occur?

   A. Electrons flow from A to B
   B. Electrons flow from B to A
   C. Protons flow from A to B
   D. Protons flow from B to A

10. Rectifiers are LEAST often made from which one of the following elements?

    A. Si   B. Ge   C. Se   D. Cu

11. Which of the following is GENERALLY used to convert a galvanometer to an ammeter?

    A. Capacitor   B. Inductor
    C. Oscillator   D. Resistor

12. The tuned circuits of a radio receiver consist BASICALLY of which one of the pairs of components below?

    A. Rectifier and antenna
    B. Tube or transistor and coil
    C. Potentiometer and oscillator
    D. Capacitor and coil

13. Often a 2-ohm and a 4-ohm resistor are connected to a 12-volt battery in series. The number of amperes flowing through the 2-ohm resistor is

    A. 0.5   B. 1   C. 2   D. 6

14. A radio wave 6 meters long will have a frequency CLOSEST to which one of the following?

    A. 6 cycles   B. 6 kilocycles
    C. 6 megacycles   D. 50 megacycles

15. Which one of the instruments below sometimes uses an internal battery?

    A. Ammeter   B. Voltmeter
    C. Wattmeter   D. Ohmmeter

16. Which one of the following kinds of rays is bent MOST by a magnetic field?

    A. Alpha   B. Beta   C. Gamma   D. Cosmic

17. A battery having an emf of 6.0 volts and an internal resistance of 0.20 ohms is being The charging current is 10 amperes.
    The potential difference at the terminals of the battery is, in volts, which one of the following?

A. 4.0 B. 5.8 C. 6.0 D. 8.0

18. Whenever magnetic lines of force are cut by a conductor,

    A. an induced current results
    B. a magnetic field is induced
    C. an emf is induced
    D. the motion will be opposed by an induced magnetic field

18.____

19. The oil drop experiment performed by Robert Millikan was used to measure

    A. energy of emitted photoelectrons
    B. charge of an electron
    C. thin film interference
    D. surface tension of oil

19.____

20. Of the following, a dielectric is MOST similar to a(n)

    A. conductor   B. capacitor
    C. inductor   D. insulator

20.____

21. To measure the electric power consumed by a direct current circuit, the MINIMUM apparatus required is a(n)

    A. ammeter   B. voltmeter
    C. ammeter and a voltmeter   D. ohmmeter

21.____

22. An AC circuit has a capacitive reactance of 100 ohms, an inductive reactance of 100 ohms, and a resistance of 100 ohms.
    The impedance, in ohms, of the circuit is

    A. 33.3   B. 100   C. 150   D. 300

22.____

23. A series electric circuit consists of a 20 ohm resistor, a 10 volt battery, and a switch.
    If the switch is closed for 6 seconds, the energy consumed by the circuit, in joules, is

    A. 10   B. 20   C. 30   D. 40

23.____

24. A 10 ohm resistor and a 50 ohm resistor are connected in parallel.
    If the current in the 10 ohm resistor is 5 amperes, the current, in amperes, in the 50 ohm resistor will be

    A. 1   B. 5   C. 25   D. 50

24.____

25. Assuming a core of adequate size, of the following, the MOST powerful electromagnet would have _____ turns and draw _____ amperes.

    A. 100; 6   B. 50; 13   C. 200; 2   D. 150; 5

25.____

26. Resistors of 2 ohms, 4 ohms, and 6 ohms are connected in series to a 24 volt battery.
    The current, in amps, through the 4 ohm resistor is

    A. 2   B. 4   C. 6   D. 22

26.____

27. An electric circuit consisting of a 10V battery and two resistors connected in series has 5 amperes of current. If a 5 microfarad capacitor is placed in series with the resistors, the current after a few minutes will be

27.____

A. 5 amperes B. more than 5 amperes
C. between 1 and 5 amperes D. zero

28. Resistance CANNOT be measured if the only instruments available are a voltmeter and a(n)

    A. ammeter B. Wheatstone Bridge
    C. galvanometer D. ohmmeter

29. In the absence of external magnetic fields, ground state electronic energy levels depend ALMOST ENTIRELY on the quantum numbers

    A. n and m_l B. n and l C. m_l and m_s D. l and m_s

30. A small object having a charge of -2 microcoulombs is placed in a uniform electric field of 10 volts/meter.
    The force, in micronewtons, on the object due to the electric field is

    A. 0.2   B. 5.0   C. 8.0   D. 20.0

31. A 50 microfarad capacitor is fully charged by a 100 volt power supply.
    The electric energy, in joules, stored in the capacitor is

    A. 0.25   B. 0.50   C. 1.50   D. 5.00

32. A thin-walled, hollow metal sphere has a diameter of 2.0 meters and is given a charge of +9 microcoulombs.
    The electric potential 8.0 meters above the top of the sphere, in volts, is

    A. 80   B. 1000   C. 1200   D. 9000

33. Assume that a length of wire having a resistance of 20 ohms is cut into four equal lengths. The four resistors then are connected in parallel with each other and their resistance measured.
    The resistance, in ohms, will be

    A. 1.25   B. 2.50   C. 5   D. 10

34. Two adjacent turns in a helical coil through which a constant current is passing will

    A. repel each other
    B. attract each other
    C. have no effect on each other
    D. have a voltage induced in them

35. When several capacitors are connected in series and to a source of direct current, each capacitor must have the same

    A. voltage B. dielectric strength
    C. charge D. capacitance

36. The current in an alternating current circuit is equal to the voltage multiplied by the

    A. impedance B. admittance
    C. capacitance D. inductance

37. The penetrating power of the x-rays produced by a Coolidge x-ray tube can be increased by increasing the

    A. number of electrons emitted from the filament
    B. distance between cathode and anode
    C. mass of the anode
    D. voltage between cathode and anode

38. A shunt motor having an armature whose resistance is 0.5 ohm is attached to a 120 volt supply. The armature current at full speed is 10 amperes.
    The back EMF, in volts, will be

    A. 5   B. 10   C. 115   D. 125

39. An electron stream sent horizontally through a magnetic field whose lines of force are horizontal and at right angles to the electron stream will

    A. curve in a horizontal plane
    B. curve in a vertical plane
    C. curve in a plane neither horizontal nor vertical
    D. pass through without curving

40. In a series wound DC electrical generator, the current in the line is

    A. the same as the field current
    B. half the current through either brush
    C. twice the current through either brush
    D. independent of the field current

41. The MOST economical 0,1 mfd condenser to be used, without danger of shorting, on a 250 volt AC line is one whose DC working voltage is rated at

    A. 250   B. 300   C. 400   D. 600

42. As the frequency of an alternating EMF in a given circuit increases, the current in the circuit at first increases, then decreases.
    The circuit contains

    A. only capacitative reactance
    B. only inductive reactance
    C. both capacitative and inductive reactance
    D. a constant impedance

43. A storage cell is connected in series with a resistance of 0.3 ohms.
    If the resistance of the cell is 0.2 ohms and its EMF is 2.5 volts, the current, expressed in amperes, in the circuit is

    A. 1/5   B. 5   C. 7.5   D. 12.5

44. A condenser of capacitance C is charged to a potential V by a quantity of charge Q.
    The energy stored in the condenser is

    A. 1/2CV   B. $1/2CV^2$ C. CV   D. $1/2CQ^2$

45. Two 50-watt, 120-volt heaters are connected in parallel to a 120-volt DC line. The power consumption is now X times as great as it would be if they were connected in series. Assuming no change in resistance, X will be

   A. 2   B. 1/2   C. 1/4   D. 4

46. The wire in the primary of a step-up transformer is usually of larger diameter than the wire in the secondary because the primary has the higher

   A. voltage
   C. current
   B. resistance
   D. number of turns

47. A spark coil operated in the classroom can produce a spark about 2 inches long. This represents a voltage of about

   A. 400   B. 4000   C. 40,000   D. 400,000

48. A substance with a magnetic permeability less than one is called

   A. ferromagnetic
   C. paramagnetic
   B. diamagnetic
   D. isomagnetic

49. The constant current in a simple series circuit is 5 amperes and the resistance of the circuit is 10 ohms. The circuit is closed for exactly 4 minutes.
   During this time, the net quantity of electricity transferred past any cross-section of the circuit is, in coulombs,

   A. 20   B. 120   C. 200   D. 1200

50. The Curie point is the

   A. temperature at which a magnetic substance loses its magnetism
   B. temperature above which a gas cannot be liquefied by pressure
   C. pressure needed to inhibit radioactivity
   D. temperature at which the addition of heat causes contraction

KEY (CORRECT ANSWERS)

1. C	11. D	21. C	31. B	41. C
2. C	12. D	22. B	32. C	42. C
3. B	13. C	23. C	33. A	43. B
4. C	14. D	24. A	34. B	44. B
5. C	15. D	25. D	35. C	45. D
6. D	16. B	26. A	36. B	46. C
7. A	17. D	27. D	37. D	47. C
8. B	18. C	28. C	38. C	48. B
9. A	19. B	29. A	39. B	49. D
10. D	20. D	30. D	40. A	50. A

EXAMINATION SECTION
TEST 1

DIRECTIONS: Each question or incomplete statement is followed by several suggested answers or completions. Select the one that BEST answers the question or completes the statement. *PRINT THE LETTER OF THE CORRECT ANSWER IN THE SPACE AT THE RIGHT.*

1. A shunt motor having an armature whose resistance is 0.5 ohm is attached to a 120 volt supply. The armature current at full speed is 10 amperes.
   The back EMF, in volts, will be

   A. 5   B. 10   C. 115   D. 125

2. An electron stream sent horizontally through a magnetic field whose lines of force are horizontal and at right angles to the electron stream will

   A. curve in a horizontal plane
   B. curve in a vertical plane
   C. curve in a plane neither horizontal nor vertical
   D. pass through without curving

3. In a series wound DC electrical generator, the current in the line is

   A. the same as the field current
   B. half the current through either brush
   C. twice the current through either brush
   D. independent of the field current

4. The MOST economical 0.1 mfd condenser to be used without danger of shorting on a 250-volt AC line is one whose DC working voltage is rated at

   A. 250   B. 300   C. 400   D. 600

5. As the frequency of an alternating EMF in a given circuit increases, the current in the circuit at first increases then decreases.
   The circuit contains

   A. only capacitative reactance
   B. only inductive reactance
   C. both capacitative and inductive reactance
   D. a constant impedance

6. A storage cell is connected in series with a resistance of 0.3 ohms.
   If the resistance of the cell is 0.2 ohms and its EMF is 2.5 volts, the current, in amperes, in the circuit is

   A. 1/5   B. 5   C. 7.5   D. 12.5

7. A condenser of capacitance C is charged to a potential V by a quantity of charge Q.
   The energy stored in the condenser is

   A. $1/2 CV$ B. $1/2 CV^2$ C. CV D. $1/2 CQ^2$

8. In the transistor, the impurities in the crystals that are GENERALLY used are

   A. osmium and cerium
   B. silicon and germanium
   C. cadmium and strontium
   D. boron and phosphorus

9. A galvanometer having an armature coil with a resistance of 10 ohms requires .01 amperes for a full-scale deflection.
   To convert this galvanometer to a voltmeter which will give a full-scale deflection when the voltage is 120 volts, a coil in series must be added that will have a resistance, in ohms, of

   A. 120   B. 1200   C. 1210   D. 11,990

10. A given length of copper wire has a resistance of 16 ohms. An equal length of copper wire having 4 times the diameter of the given wire will have a resistance of _____ ohm(s).

    A. 1   B. 4   C. 16   D. 64

11. A battery has an open circuit voltage of 20 volts and an internal resistance of 0.25 ohm. When it delivers a current of 10 amperes, the terminal voltage will be

    A. 15   B. 17.5   C. 18   D. 20

12. The energy converted into heat during a cycle of a hysteresis loop was formulated by

    A. Steinmetz   B. Edison   C. Hertz   D. Maxwell

13. Assume that the movable coil of a D'Arsonval type of voltmeter that has a resistance of 300 ohms and a current of 0.02 ampere will give a full-scale reading.
    The series resistance, in ohms, needed to construct a voltmeter with a full scale of 150 volts is

    A. 7200   B. 8100   C. 7800   D. 7500

14. An alternating voltage is supplied to a circuit consisting of an incandescent lamp and a coil of many turns.
    The current in the circuit

    A. lags behind the voltage
    B. leads the voltage
    C. is in phase with the voltage
    D. is rectified into direct current

15. A series circuit with resistance of 40 ohms, inductive reactance of 75 ohms, and capacitive reactance of 45 ohms is connected to a 150 volt AC source.
    The impedance of the circuit is, in ohms,

    A. 30   B. 40   C. 50   D. 70

16. If the charge on a single electron is 1.60×10^{-19} coulombs, then an electron volt is 1.60×10^{-19}

    A. joule
    B. /300 joule
    C. x 300 joule
    D. erg

17. Three resistors each of 12 ohms, connected in parallel with each other, are connected in series to a resistor of 6 ohms, and to a 60 volt source.
    The current, in amperes, through the 6 ohms resistor will be

    A. 5　　B. 6　　C. 10　　D. 15

17.____

18. Two electrical condensers having capacitances of 9 and 18 microfarads, respectively, are connected in series.
    The capacitance, in microfarads, of the two connected together will be

    A. 6　　B. 9　　C. 13.5　　D. 27

18.____

19. The current in a coil having an inductance of 32 millihenries increases in magnitude from 2 to 6 amperes in 0.05 second.
    The voltage of self-induction will equal

    A. 1.28　　B. 1.60　　C. 1.92　　D. 2.56

19.____

20. A variable electrical condenser of the type used in radio sets is completely immersed in oil whose dielectric strength is 3.5.
    As compared to its former state, its

    A. ability to withstand high voltages has been reduced
    B. capacitance has been increased
    C. capacitance has been decreased
    D. capacitance remains unaffected

20.____

21. The number of calories a 20-ohm electric heater operating under a potential difference of 120 volts develops in one second is APPROXIMATELY

    A. 120　　B. 175　　C. 240　　D. 720

21.____

22. An alternating current whose effective value is 100 amperes will have a peak value, in amperes, of

    A. 110　　B. 125　　C. 136　　D. 141

22.____

23. An alternating voltage is supplied to a circuit containing a capacitance C, an inductance L, and a resistance R in series with each other.
    The resonant frequency is increased by

    A. increasing L　　　　B. increasing C
    C. decreasing R　　　　D. decreasing C

23.____

24. When resonance occurs in a circuit supplied with an alternating voltage, the

    A. capacitance equals the inductance
    B. inductance equals the reciprocal of the capacitance
    C. inductive reactance equals the capacitative reactance
    D. impedance equals zero

24.____

25. A coil with a potential difference of 20 volts across its ends develops heat at the rate of 800 calories per second. The resistance of the coil, in ohms, is

    A. 0.12　　B. 1.20　　C. 4.00　　D. 40.0

25.____

26. In a selenium rectifier, current flow practically ceases when the

   A. selenium becomes negative
   B. selenium becomes positive
   C. accompanying alloy becomes negative
   D. applied voltage exceeds the critical value

27. An alternating current generator having 4 poles rotates at 60 revolutions per second. The frequency of the current produced, in cycles per second, is

   A. 60   B. 15   C. 120   D. 240

28. If an AC circuit contains resistance only, then current

   A. and voltage are in phase
   B. lags by 45°
   C. leads by 90°
   D. lags by 45° and voltage leads by 45°

29. A galvanometer has a resistance of 50 ohms and requires 0.05 amperes for full-scale deflection.
   The voltage required for half-scale deflection is

   A. 0.001   B. 0.05   C. 1.25   D. 2.5

30. If the capacitance in an oscillator circuit of frequency F is increased fourfold, the frequency of the oscillator becomes

   A. F/4   B. F/2   C. 2F   D. 4F

31. In circuit A, one ampere of AC flows for 1 hour and generates X calories. In circuit B, one ampere of DC flows for 1 hour.
   The heat generated in circuit B is

   A. 0.707X
   B. the same as in A
   C. $\dfrac{X}{0.707}$
   D. 0.24IRT

32. A 2 and a 4 ohm resistor are connected in series and the combination is connected in parallel to a 6 ohm resistor. The TOTAL resistance, in ohms, is

   A. 1.2   B. 3   C. 9   D. 12

33. The Compton effect is MOST important for its contribution to our knowledge regarding the nature of

   A. radiation
   B. neutrons
   C. protons
   D. crystal lattice structure

34. The GREATEST number of 100-watt, 110-volt electric lights that can be used simultaneously on a household line (110 volts) without burning out the 15-ampere fuse is

   A. 6   B. 10   C. 16   D. 30

35. The current in the armature of a generator equipped with a commutator is

   A. alternating
   B. intermittent direct
   C. pulsating direct
   D. uniform direct

36. Eddy currents in the core of a transformer may be MINIMIZED by constructing the core of

   A. laminated iron sheets in electrical contact with each other
   B. laminated iron sheets insulated from each other
   C. solid soft steel
   D. solid hard steel

37. When 60 cycle alternating voltage is applied to a diode, the current flowing through is _____ current.

   A. 30 cycle alternating
   B. 60 cycle alternating
   C. steady direct
   D. pulsating direct

38. The earth inductor compass uses a circular coil rotating in the earth's magnetic field. MAXIMUM induced EMF will be induced when the axis of rotation is always

   A. horizontal
   B. vertical
   C. perpendicular to the magnetic field
   D. parallel to the magnetic field

39. An electric broiler has two resistors, equal in resistance, that may be connected in series or parallel by a switch.
    Assuming that the line voltage is constant, the heat produced by the series connection as compared to the parallel connection will be in the ratio of

   A. 1:4   B. 4:1   C. 1:2   D. 2:1

40. Three resistors of 5, 10, and 15 ohms are joined in parallel to a 120V circuit.
    The equivalent resistance of this circuit, in ohms, is

   A. less than 5
   B. between 5 and 10
   C. between 10 and 15
   D. more than 15

41. A 22-volt battery has an internal resistance of 1.5 ohms. When used to supply a lamp drawing a current of 2 amperes, a voltmeter across the battery will read

   A. 3   B. 19   C. 22   D. 25

42. An electron current flowing from north to south in a wire will deflect the north pole of a compass held above it

   A. toward the east
   B. toward the west
   C. upward
   D. downward

43. A capacitor, a resistor, and an inductance are connected in series. The frequency of an applied alternating voltage is varied until the circuit is in resonance with it.
    The current in the circuit will

   A. be minimum in value
   B. be in phase with the impressed voltage

C. lead the voltage by 90°
D. lag the voltage by 90°

44. The constant current in a simple series circuit is 5 amperes and the resistance of the circuit is 10 ohms. The circuit is closed for exactly 4 minutes.
During this time, the net quantity of electricity transferred past any cross-section of the circuit is, in coulombs,

   A. 20   B. 120   C. 200   D. 1200

45. If a step-down transformer is 100% efficient, the primary and secondary coils will have the same number of

   A. amperes   B. volts   C. watts   D. turns

46. When a person speaks into a telephone transmitter, the current in the primary circuit is

   A. alternating   B. pulsating direct
   C. reduced to zero   D. steady direct

47. To convert alternating current to direct current, one may use a(n)

   A. commutator   B. transformer
   C. electrostatic machine D. induction coil

48. Kilowatt-hours may be converted into

   A. ft-lb   B. ft-lb/sec
   C. lb/sq. in.   D. lb/cu. ft.

49. The combined resistance of two 12-ohm resistors connected in series is _____ ohms.

   A. 6   B. 12   C. 24   D. 144

50. The core of an electromagnet should be made of

   A. silver   B. soft iron
   C. steel   D. tungsten

KEY (CORRECT ANSWERS)

1. C	11. B	21. B	31. B	41. B
2. B	12. A	22. D	32. B	42. A
3. A	13. A	23. D	33. A	43. B
4. C	14. A	24. C	34. C	44. D
5. C	15. C	25. A	35. A	45. C
6. B	16. D	26. A	36. B	46. B
7. B	17. B	27. C	37. D	47. A
8. D	18. A	28. A	38. C	48. A
9. D	19. D	29. C	39. A	49. C
10. A	20. B	30. B	40. A	50. B

TEST 2

DIRECTIONS: Each question or incomplete statement is followed by several suggested answers or completions. Select the one that BEST answers the question or completes the statement. *PRINT THE LETTER OF THE CORRECT ANSWER IN THE SPACE AT THE RIGHT.*

1. The potential expressed in e.s.u. at a point midway between two equal positive charges of 50 statcoulombs (e.s.u.) placed 10 cm apart is

   A. +4   B. +5   C. +10   D. +20

2. Eddy currents in the core of a transformer may be minimized by constructing the core of

   A. laminated iron sheets in electrical contact with each other
   B. laminated iron sheets insulated from each other
   C. solid soft steel
   D. solid hard steel

3. When 60 cycle alternating voltage is applied to a diode, the current flowing through is _____ current.

   A. 30 cycle alternating   B. 60 cycle alternating
   C. steady direct   D. pulsating direct

4. The earth inductor compass uses a circular coil rotating in the earth's magnetic field. Maximum induced EMF will be induced when the axis of rotation is always

   A. horizontal
   B. vertical
   C. perpendicular to the magnetic field
   D. parallel to the magnetic field

5. An electric broiler has two resistors, equal in resistance, that may be connected in series or parallel by a switch.
   Assuming that the line voltage is constant, the heat produced by the series connection as compared to the parallel connection will be in the ratio of

   A. 1:4   B. 4:1   C. 1:2   D. 2:1

6. Three resistors of 5, 10, and 15 ohms are joined in parallel to a 120V circuit. The equivalent resistance of this circuit, in ohms, is

   A. less than 5   B. between 5 and 10
   C. between 10 and 15   D. more than 15

7. A 22-volt battery has an internal resistance of 1.5 ohms. When used to supply a lamp drawing a current of 2 amperes, a voltmeter across the battery will read

   A. 3   B. 19   C. 22   D. 25

8. An electron current flowing from north to south in a wire will deflect the north pole of a compass held above it

   A. toward the east   B. toward the west
   C. upward   D. downward

9. A capacitor, a resistor, and an inductance are connected in series. The frequency of an applied alternating voltage is varied until the circuit is in resonance with it.
   The current in the circuit will

   A. be minimum in value
   B. be in phase with the impressed voltage
   C. lead the voltage by 90°
   D. lag the voltage by 90°

10. A 2 and a 4 ohm resistor are connected in series and the combination is connected in parallel to a 6 ohm resistor. The TOTAL resistance, in ohms, is

    A. 1.2   B. 3   C. 9   D. 12

11. The Compton effect is MOST important for its contribution to our knowledge regarding the nature of

    A. radiation
    C. protons
    B. neutrons
    D. crystal lattice structure

12. Assume that the movable coil of a D'Arsonval type of voltmeter has a resistance of 300 ohms and a current of 0.02 ampere will give a full-scale reading.
    The series resistance, in ohms, needed to construct a voltmeter with a full scale of 150 volts is

    A. 7200   B. 8100   C. 7800   D. 7500

13. An alternating voltage is supplied to a circuit consisting of an incandescent lamp and a coil of many turns.
    The current in the circuit

    A. lags behind the voltage
    B. leads the voltage
    C. is in phase with the voltage
    D. is rectified into direct current

14. The number of calories a 20-ohm electric heater operating under a potential difference of 120 volts develops in one second is APPROXIMATELY

    A. 120   B. 175   C. 240   D. 720

15. An alternating current whose effective value of 100 amperes will have a peak value, in amperes, of

    A. 110   B. 125   C. 136   D. 141

16. By inductively feeding back energy from the plate circuit into the grid circuit, a triode may be used as a(n)

    A. demodulator
    C. detector
    B. amplifier
    D. diode

17. When a current of 2 amperes flows through a conductor of 2 ohms resistance for 3 seconds, the heat produced, in joules, is

    A. 12   B. 24   C. 36   D. 72

18. A length of wire, diameter 2 mils, has a resistance of 6 ohms.
    The same length of wire of the same material having a diameter of 4 mils has a resistance, in ohms, of

    A. 1.5   B. 3   C. 12   D. 24

19. The generalization that the algebraic sum of the currents at a junction in a circuit equals zero was postulated by

    A. Ohm   B. Kirchhoff   C. Onnes   D. Seebeck

20. It is desired to charge an electroscope negatively by induction.
    One of the steps that must be performed is to

    A. use a negatively charged rod
    B. remove positive charges
    C. remove electrons
    D. ground the electroscope

21. A series AC circuit contains an inductance L, a capacitance C, and a resistor R.
    The impedance of this circuit equals

    A. $R^2 + X_L + X_C$
    B. $\sqrt{R^2 + (X_L - X_C)^2}$
    C. $R^2 + \sqrt{X_L - X_C}$
    D. $R^2 - X_L - X_C^2$

22. In an AC circuit in which the current and voltage are out of phase by 90°, an ammeter reads 2 and a voltmeter reads 120.
    The power expended by this circuit, in watts, equals

    A. zero   B. 60   C. 120   D. 240

23. A voltmeter showed a reading, when connected to a circuit carrying a sinusoidal alternating current, of 100 volts (RMS value).
    The MAXIMUM instantaneous voltage was

    A. 100   B. 141   C. 173   D. 200

24. A condenser of capacitance C is charged to a potential V by a quantity of charge Q.
    The energy stored in the condenser is

    A. 1/2CV   B. 1/2CV²   C. CV   D. 1/2CQ²

25. Two 50-watt, 120-volt heaters are connected in parallel to a 120-volt DC line. The power consumption is now X times as great as it would be if they were connected in series. Assuming no change in resistance, X will be

    A. 2   B. 1/2   C. 1/4   D. 4

26. The wire in the primary of a step-up transformer is USUALLY of larger diameter than the wire in the secondary because the primary has the higher

    A. voltage   B. resistance
    C. current   D. number of turns

4 (#2)

27. A spark coil operated in the classroom can produce a spark about 2 inches long. This represents a voltage of about

    A. 400   B. 4000   C. 40,000   D. 400,000

    27._____

28. A substance with a magnetic permeability less than one is called

    A. ferromagnetic   B. diamagnetic
    C. paramagnetic   D. isomagnetic

    28._____

29. The constant current in a simple series circuit is 5 amperes and the resistance of the circuit is 10 ohms. The circuit is closed for exactly 4 minutes.
    During this time, the net quantity of electricity transferred past any cross-section of the circuit is, in coulombs,

    A. 20   B. 120   C. 200   D. 1200

    29._____

30. The Curie point is the

    A. temperature at which a magnetic substance loses its magnetism
    B. temperature above which a gas cannot be liquefied by pressure
    C. pressure needed to inhibit radioactivity
    D. temperature at which the addition of heat causes contraction

    30._____

31. A 0-10 milliampere meter has a resistance of 20 ohms. To convert this meter to an ammeter with a range of 0-1 ampere, one should connect a resistance of APPROXIMATELY

    A. 1/5 ohm in parallel   B. 200 ohms in series
    C. 2000 ohms in parallel   D. 2000 ohms in series

    31._____

32. An alternating voltage is supplied to a circuit containing a capacitance C, an inductance L, and a resistance R in series with each other.
    The resonant frequency is increased by

    A. increasing L   B. increasing C
    C. decreasing R   D. decreasing C

    32._____

33. When resonance occurs in a circuit supplied with an alternating voltage, the

    A. capacitance equals the inductance
    B. inductance equals the reciprocal of the capacitance
    C. inductive reactance equals the capacitative reactance
    D. impedance equals zero

    33._____

34. The phase angle in an alternating current circuit is zero degrees when the circuit

    A. contains resistance *only*
    B. contains inductance *only*
    C. contains capacitance *only*
    D. is not closed

    34._____

35. When a capacitor of 10 microfarads capacity is connected to a 100 volt current source, the charge acquired by the capacitor will have a magnitude, in coulombs, of

    A. 10^{-6} B. 10^{-4} C. 10^2 D. 10^3

    35._____

36. The efficiency in percent of a one horsepower motor drawing 8.0 amperes at 125 volts is APPROXIMATELY   36.____

    A. 60	B. 75	C. 85	D. 90

37. The product of the pole strength of a bar magnet and the distance between the poles is called the magnetic   37.____

    A. moment	B. flux
    C. field intensity	D. reluctance

38. Assume that a length of wire having a resistance of 20 ohms is cut into four equal lengths. The four resistors then are connected in parallel with each other and their resistance measured.   38.____
    The resistance, in ohms, will be

    A. 1.25	B. 2.50	C. 5	D. 10

39. Two adjacent turns in a helical coil through which a constant current is passing will   39.____

    A. repel each other
    B. attract each other
    C. have no effect on each other
    D. have a voltage induced in them

40. When several capacitors are connected in series and to a source of direct current, each capacitor must have the SAME   40.____

    A. voltage	B. dielectric strength
    C. charge	D. capacitance

41. The current in an alternating current circuit is equal to the voltage multiplied by   41.____

    A. the impedance	B. admittance
    C. capacitance	D. inductance

42. Three identical resistors connected in parallel have a total resistance of 10 ohms. If these resistors are separated and then connected to each other in series, the TOTAL resistance, in ohms, will be   42.____

    A. 3.3	B. 10.0	C. 30.0	D. 90.0

43. A transformer has 100 turns in its primary winding and 1000 turns in its secondary winding.   43.____
    If a 1.5 volt dry cell is connected across the primary winding, the steady state voltage across the secondary winding will be

    A. 15 volts AC	B. 15 volts DC
    C. 0.15 volts DC	D. zero

44. A long wire at a constant height above the ground is carrying electron current from the east to the west.   44.____
    The direction of the magnetic field, due to the current, at a point on the ground directly under the wire is

    A. north	B. south	C. up	D. down

45. A 9-volt battery is connected to an 18 ohm resistor.
If the internal resistance of the battery is 9 ohms, the current in the circuit, in amperes, is

   A. 1/3   B. 1/2   C. 3   D. 36

46. An electric circuit carries a current of 2.0 amperes.
The quantity of electric charge that passes a given point in the circuit in 6.0 seconds, in coulombs, is

   A. 1.5   B. 2.0   C. 3.0   D. 12.0

47. A 10 microfarad parallel plate capacitor is modified by doubling the area of its plates and doubling the distance between the plates.
The capacitance, in microfarads, after modification is

   A. 5   B. 10   C. 20   D. 40

48. A straight horizontal wire 3 meters long and carrying a current of 4 amperes is in a uniform vertical magnetic field having a strength of 5 tesla.
The force, in newtons, exerted by the magnetic field on the wire is

   A. 2.4   B. 6.7   C. 12.0   D. 60.0

49. If the impedance of a 110 volt circuit is 44 ohms, the current, in amperes, flowing in the circuit will be

   A. 0.25   B. 0.4   C. 2.5   D. 66.0

50. If a 120-volt AC source is connected to a 10 ohm resistance, a 10 ohm inductive reactance, and a 10 ohm capacitive reactance all in series, the resultant current, in amperes, is

   A. 3.1   B. 4.0   C. 4.4   D. 12.0

KEY (CORRECT ANSWERS)

1. D	11. A	21. B	31. A	41. B
2. B	12. A	22. A	32. D	42. C
3. D	13. A	23. B	33. C	43. B
4. C	14. B	24. B	34. A	44. A
5. A	15. D	25. D	35. B	45. A
6. A	16. B	26. C	36. B	46. D
7. B	17. B	27. C	37. A	47. D
8. A	18. A	28. B	38. A	48. D
9. B	19. B	29. D	39. B	49. C
10. B	20. D	30. A	40. C	50. D

EXAMINATION SECTION
TEST 1

DIRECTIONS: Each question or incomplete statement is followed by several suggested answers or completions. Select the one that BEST answers the question or completes the statement. *PRINT THE LETTER OF THE CORRECT ANSWER IN THE SPACE AT THE RIGHT.*

1. Two lamps need 50V and 2 amp each in order to operate at a desired brilliancy. If they are to be connected in series across a 120V line, the resistance, in ohms, of the rheostat that must be placed in series with the lamps needs to be
    A. 4 B. 10 C. 20 D. 100

2. The Kelvin Bridge is BASICALLY a device for measuring
    A. low resistance
    B. high resistance
    C. high emf
    D. low emf

3. If a capacitance of 250 Mf, connected to an AC line, has a capacitive reactance measured at 10.6 ohms, the AC line has a frequency, in c/sec, of
    A. 30 B. 60 C. 90 D. 120

4. Of the following, the one that is NOT normally used as a component of some electronic oscillator circuits is the
    A. lighthouse tube
    B. pitot tube
    C. klystron
    D. magnetron

5. The term *magnetostriction* refers to the
    A. strict conditions that determine magnetic polarity
    B. change in dimensions when a substance is magnetized
    C. Curie point
    D. magnetic properties near absolute zero

6. In a three-phase alternator, the armature is Y-connected and three terminals are brought out.
   If the voltage per armature phase is 200V, the line voltage is CLOSEST to which one of the following?
    A. 140V B. 170V C. 340V D. 400V

7. If a charged capacitor loses one-half its charge by leakage, it has lost what fraction of its store of energy?
    A. 1/8 B. 1/4 C. 1/2 D. 3/4

8. An electrical current flows through an iron wire connected in series with another iron wire of equal length but one-half its cross-section area.
   If the voltage drop across the thicker wire is 8 volts, the drop across the thinner wire, in volts, is CLOSEST to
    A. 2 B. 4 C. 8 D. 16

2 (#1)

9. Of the following connections, the one which may be used to convert a galvanometer into a voltmeter is that of a _____-ohm resistor in _____.   9.____

    A. .005; series   B. .005; parallel
    C. 5000; series   D. 5000; parallel

10. A pivoted compass needle placed directly beneath a horizontal wire carrying an electrical current will orient itself so that its   10.____

    A. long axis is parallel to the wire
    B. long axis is perpendicular to the wire
    C. north pole will point downward
    D. north pole will point upward

11. The element of an n-p-n transistor which is analogous to the grid of a vacuum tube is the   11.____

    A. base   B. collector
    C. emitter   D. suppressor

12. An example of a transducer is a   12.____

    A. transistor   B. telephone transmitter
    C. transformer   D. thermionic tube

13. In a parallel electrical circuit, the device with the LOWEST resistance has the   13.____

    A. least heating effect   B. highest wattage
    C. lowest current   D. lowest voltage drop

14. A device known as a transducer is used to convert   14.____

    A. AC to DC and back again
    B. a light beam into sound
    C. heat waves into sound pressure and back again
    D. sound pressure to electric signals and back again

15. Two resistances of 6 and 24 ohms are connected in series to a 120-volt source. The voltage drop across the 6 ohm resistor is   15.____

    A. 4   B. 18   C. 24   D. 96

16. Four capacitors, each of 10 microfarads capacity, are fully charged when connected in parallel.
The TOTAL equivalent capacity of this combination, in microfarads, is   16.____

    A. 2.5   B. 10   C. 14   D. 40

17. The peak voltage of an alternating emf is 141 volts. The EFFECTIVE value of the voltage, in volts, is   17.____

    A. 70.5   B. 100   C. 141   D. 200

18. In a step-down transformer, the secondary winding is usually thicker than the primary winding because the secondary has the HIGHER   18.____

    A. current   B. wattage
    C. voltage   D. resistance

19. A 100-watt lamp is able to generate more light and heat than a 60-watt lamp because the 100-watt lamp

    A. draws less current
    B. is usually operated at a higher voltage
    C. usually uses a different filament material
    D. has less resistance

20. Three ideal components: a resistor, an inductor, and a capacitor, are connected in series to a source of AC. The potential difference across each component is 40 volts. The TOTAL voltage across the three components is

    A. zero B. $40\sqrt{2}V$ C. 40V D. 120V

21. The potential difference across a 6-ohm resistor is 6 volts. The power used by the resistor is, in watts,

    A. 6 B. 12 C. 18 D. 24

22. In a sinusoidal alternating current, the peak value of the current equals

    A. the effective value of the current
    B. 0.707 times the effective value of the current
    C. 1.41 times the effective value of the current
    D. 0.707 times the peak value of the emf divided by the resistance

23. Electrical resistance is equivalent to which one of the following?

    A. Work/charge
    B. Work • time/charge
    C. Work • time/charge^2
    D. Work • time/current

24. At 60 cycles per second, a coil has an inductive reactance of 100 ohms and a certain capacitor has a capacitive reactance of 400 ohms.
    At what frequency, in cy/sec, will the two devices have the SAME reactance?

    A. 30 B. 120 C. 180 D. 240

25. Which one of the following purposes may be served by a diode in a vacuum tube circuit?

    A. Amplifier   B. Condenser
    C. Resistor   D. Detector

26. In a series-wound motor, the current present in the armature winding is _____ is applied to the motor.

    A. DC even when AC   B. DC when DC
    C. AC only when AC   D. AC even when DC

27. The electromotive force, in volts, of 4 fresh similar dry cells, connected in parallel, is usually CLOSEST to which one of the following?

    A. 1.5 B. 3 C. 4.5 D. 6

28. An alternating current generator differs from a direct current generator by having

    A. splip-rings   B. brushes
    C. a split-ring commutator D. an armature

29. The GREATEST number of 100 watt lamps which can be connected in parallel in a 120 volt system without blowing a 10 ampere fuse is   29.____

    A. 12 B. 18 C. 24 D. 30

30. The construction of a direct current motor is basically the SAME as that of a(n)   30.____

    A. direct current generator
    B. alternating current motor
    C. alternating current generator
    D. ballistic galvanometer

31. A galvanometer may be used as an ammeter by   31.____

    A. shunting the galvanometer with a high resistance
    B. connecting a low resistance in parallel with the galvanometer
    C. connecting a low resistance in series
    D. connecting a high resistance in series

32. Resistances of 20 ohms and 60 ohms are connected in parallel to a generator. If the current in the 60 ohm resistance is 1 ampere, the current in the 20 ohm resistance will be _____ ampere(s).   32.____

    A. 1 B. 1/3 C. 2/3 D. 3

33. Direct current may be changed to alternating current by the use of a   33.____

    A. transformer   B. rectifier
    C. spark coil   D. diode

34. Iron and copper wires of equal lengths and cross-sections are connected in series. During the passage of current through the wires for a period of two minutes, the   34.____

    A. voltage drop across the copper will be larger than across the iron
    B. current through the copper will be greater than that through the iron
    C. current through the iron will be greater than that through the copper
    D. heat generated in the iron will be greater than that in the copper

35. If the current flowing through a given resistor is doubled, the amount of heat generated is multiplied by   35.____

    A. 1/2 B. 1 C. 2 D. 4

36. In wiring an electrical circuit, the laboratory assistant should make the *live* connection the _____ act in assembling and the _____ act in disassembling.   36.____

    A. last; first   B. first; first
    C. last; last   D. first; last

37. The electric current used in the school laboratory should be   37.____

    A. alternating and not direct
    B. direct and not alternating
    C. below 20 volts
    D. sent through a limiting load resistance

38. Which one of the following pairs of factors determines the direction of an induced electromotive force?
Direction of

    A. motion and direction of field
    B. motion and rate of rotation
    C. field and rate of rotation
    D. field and number of turns on coil

39. A rectifier is a device used to

    A. change direct current into alternating current
    B. increase the voltage
    C. filter out stray currents
    D. change alternating current to direct current

40. When a small quantity of a gas like mercury vapor is introduced into a diode, its net effect is to do which one of the following?

    A. Reduce plate current flow
    B. Increase the number of negative ions
    C. Increase the number of electrons reaching the plate
    D. Decrease the number of positive ions

41. The capacitive reactance of a circuit is increased by which one of the following?
A(n)

    A. increase in the frequency of the voltage
    B. decrease in the frequency of the voltage
    C. increase in the resistance of the circuit
    D. decrease in the resistance of the circuit

42. In an electrical circuit containing both inductance and capacitance, if the capacitance increases, the natural frequency of the circuit will

    A. increase
    B. decrease
    C. increase to a maximum then decrease
    D. remain constant

43. Of the following, the type of coupling in a radio circuit that is LEAST likely to introduce distortion is

    A. resistance   B. transformer
    C. impedance   D. capacitative

44. The function of the grid in a triode is to

    A. supply electrons
    B. control the plate current
    C. control the temperature of the tube
    D. control the plate voltage

45. The ESSENTIAL difference between an audio and a radio frequency transformer is the absence in the radio transformer of a(n)   45._____

   A. capacitor
   B. iron core
   C. quartz crystal
   D. transistor element

46. The PRINCIPAL effect of the space charge in a vacuum tube is to   46._____

   A. decrease the plate current
   B. increase the plate current
   C. increase the plate voltage
   D. increase the electron emission from the cathode

47. In the expression for induced emf, $V = \frac{-d\phi}{dt}$, the minus sign is a consequence of _____ Law.   47._____

   A. Coulomb's
   B. Biot-Savart
   C. Lenz's
   D. Faraday's

48. An oscillating circuit contains an inductance of 10uh, a capacitor of 5uf, and a capacitor of 25uf, all in parallel. The natural frequency of the circuit, in kilocycles/sec, is CLOSEST to which one of the following?   48._____

   A. 4.7   B. 9.2   C. 4,700   D. 9,200

49. During normal operation, AC is present in which one of the following?   49._____

   A. Armature winding of a DC motor
   B. Field winding of a DC motor
   C. Field winding of a DC generator
   D. Coil of a ballistic galvanometer

50. The emission of electrons from the surface of a heated conductor was FIRST observed by   50._____

   A. Fleming   B. Hertz   C. Armstrong   D. Edison

KEY (CORRECT ANSWERS)

1.	B	11.	A	21.	A	31.	B	41.	B
2.	A	12.	B	22.	C	32.	D	42.	B
3.	B	13.	B	23.	C	33.	C	43.	A
4.	B	14.	D	24.	B	34.	D	44.	B
5.	B	15.	C	25.	D	35.	D	45.	B
6.	C	16.	D	26.	D	36.	A	46.	A
7.	D	17.	B	27.	A	37.	D	47.	C
8.	D	18.	A	28.	A	38.	A	48.	B
9.	C	19.	D	29.	A	39.	D	49.	A
10.	B	20.	C	30.	A	40.	C	50.	D

TEST 2

DIRECTIONS: Each question or incomplete statement is followed by several suggested answers or completions. Select the one that BEST answers the question or completes the statement. *PRINT THE LETTER OF THE CORRECT ANSWER IN THE SPACE AT THE RIGHT.*

1. Lenz's Law states that the 1._____
   A. induced current is always equal in magnitude to the impressed current
   B. induced field has a direction opposite to that of the original field if this is decreasing
   C. induced field always has such direction as to aid the motion of a conductor moving in the field
   D. induced field has the same direction as the original if this is decreasing

2. A long straight wire is in a magnetic field and, when the wire carries a current of 4 amp, the magnetic field exerts on it a force per unit length equal to K. 2._____
   If the current is changed to one amp and the magnetic flux density is doubled, the force per unit length is
   A. K/8   B. K/4   C. K/2   D. K

3. In an AC series circuit, the inductive reactance, capacitive reactance, and resistance are 25 ohms each. 3._____
   When a 100 volt AC potential difference is applied, the current flow, in amperes, will equal
   A. 1.3   B. 4   C. 13   D. 2500

4. The plate current in an electron tube is initially 10 milliamperes under certain conditions. When the plate voltage is increased by 10 volts, the plate current becomes 11 milliamperes. Under the same original conditions, an increase of grid voltage of 1 volt increases the plate current to 11 milliamperes. 4._____
   The amplification factor of the tube is then
   A. 0.1   B. 10   C. 100   D. 110

5. To obtain the HIGHEST possible transformer efficiency, it would be desirable to have the 5._____
   A. turn ratio as high as possible
   B. input current low and output current high
   C. core made of solid copper
   D. hysteresis loop as narrow as possible

6. If a capacitor, 10^{-4} farad capacity, and a 1 megohm resistor are connected in series to a 100 volt battery, the time constant, in seconds, for this circuit is 6._____
   A. 10^{-2} B. 10^{-1} C. 10^2 D. 10^4

7. The impedance Z of an alternating current circuit is ALWAYS given by the formula Z = 7._____
   A. $2\pi fL$
   B. $1/2\pi fC$
   C. $2\pi fL - 1/2\pi fC$
   D. $\sqrt{R^2 + (2\pi fL - 1/2\pi fC)^2}$

8. The transmission of an electric current through an electrolyte is done by means of

   A. electrons *only*
   B. positive and negative ions
   C. positive ions *only*
   D. positive ions and electrons

9. Of the following, a device which is ALWAYS connected in parallel in a circuit is a(n)

   A. ammeter   B. fuse   C. switch   D. voltmeter

10. A diode may be used as which one of the following?

    A. Amplifier
    B. Oscillator
    C. Rectifier
    D. Transformer

11. In an n-p-n transistor used as an amplifier, which one of the following is a NECESSARY connection?
    _____ side of battery _____.

    A. Negative; A to emitter
    B. Negative; B to collector
    C. Negative; A to base
    D. Positive; B to base

12. When two 4 ohm resistors are joined in series and connected to a power supply which consists of a 7 volt battery whose positive terminal is connected to that of a 9V battery, the current flow in the resistors is, in amperes, the two free terminals being connected to the resistors,

    A. 0.25   B. 1.0   C. 2.0   D. 8.0

13. A wattmeter, when properly connected in the circuit, is connected

    A. only in series
    B. only in parallel
    C. either in series or in parallel
    D. both in series and in parallel

14. When an incandescent lamp rated at 120V, 60W draws a current of 0.5 amp, the number of electrons/sec passing through the wire is

    A. $(0.5)(6.25 \times 10^{18})$
    B. $(0.5)(1.6 \times 10^{-19})$
    C. $(60)(0.5)(1.6 \times 10^{-19})$
    D. $(60)(0.5)(6.25 \times 10^{18})$

15. When a resistor and a capacitor are connected in series to a dry cell, at the instant of closing the circuit, the

    A. voltage across the resistor is zero
    B. voltage across the capacitor is at maximum
    C. charge on the capacitor is at maximum
    D. current in the circuit is at maximum

16. An electron and a proton are accelerated from rest through a potential difference of 1000 volts.
    As a result, the ratio of the kinetic energy of the proton to that of the electron is

    A. 1:1   B. 1840:1   C. 1:1840   D. 1000:1

17. If a uniform wire 10 feet long having a resistance of 1.0 ohm is cut into 10 equal pieces which are then connected in parallel with each other, the resistance of this parallel array, expressed in ohms, is

    A. 0.010   B. 0.10   C. 1.0   D. 10

18. When a 30 volt, 60-cycle AC source is connected to a 90-ohm resistor in series with a 50 uf capacitor and a 60 millihenry inductance, the impedance of the circuit, in ohms, is CLOSEST to which one of the following?

    A. 45   B. 70   C. 95   D. 120

19. When a 10 foot length of copper wire having a resistance of 2 ohms is drawn out, with uniform thickness, to a length of 30 feet, its resistance, in ohms, will be which one of the following?

    A. 2   B. 6   C. 12   D. 18

20. The force of attraction between two opposite electric charges is 24 dynes.
    If the positive charge is doubled, and the negative charge is halved, the force of attraction will be

    A. halved   B. unchanged
    C. doubled   D. quadrupled

21. Wire A has a resistance of 1,000 ohms.
    If wire B, which is of the same material as A and at the same temperature, is twice as long as A and has a cross-sectional area 5 times that of A, the resistance of B, in ohms, will be

    A. 100   B. 400   C. 2,500   D. 10,000

22. If a 1-HP electric motor draws 4 amp when operating from a 220-volt line, the efficiency of the motor, in percent, is CLOSEST to which one of the following?

    A. 65   B. 75   C. 85   D. 95

23. Which one of the following represents, in ohms, the resistance of a 1,000-watt DC electric heater drawing a current of 10 amp?

    A. 10   B. 100   C. 900   D. 10,000

24. If a 30-volt, 60-cycle AC source is connected to a circuit containing in series a 90-ohm resistor, a 50 uf capacitor, and a 60 millihenry inductance, the tangent of the phase angle is CLOSEST to which one of the following?

    A. .17   B. .34   C. .51   D. .68

25. A circuit containing an inductance of 320 uh and a capacitance of 80 uuf will have a resonant frequency, in c/sec, CLOSEST to which one of the following?

    A. 60 B. 1×10^3 C. 1×10^4 D. 1×10^6

26. If an electric iron whose resistance is 24 ohms draws 5 amperes, what heat energy will be produced, in joules, in one hour?

    A. 2.16×10^5 B. 5.18×10^5 C. 2.16×10^6 D. 5.18×10^6

27. A galvanometer having a resistance of 50 ohms reads full scale with a current of 1 milliampere.
    To convert the galvanometer to a 10-volt voltmeter requires a multiplier whose resistance, in ohms, is

    A. 9,500 B. 9,950 C. 10,000 D. 10,050

28. When three capacitors, 8, 10, and 40 uf, respectively, are connected in series to a 300-volt DC source, the combined capacitance in the circuit, in uf, is CLOSEST to which one of the following?

    A. 4 B. 5.14 C. 29 D. 58

29. In order for a 30-volt, 90-watt lamp to work properly when inserted in a 120-volt DC line, it should have in series with it a resistor whose resistance, in ohms, is

    A. 10 B. 20 C. 30 D. 40

30. The combined resistance of two resistors (R_1 and R_2) in parallel is given by which one of the following formulas?
    $R_T=$

    A. $\dfrac{R_1+R_2}{R_1 R_2}$ B. $\dfrac{R_1 R_2}{R_1+R_2}$ C. $\dfrac{2R_1}{R_1+R_2}$ D. $\dfrac{2R_2}{R_1+R_2}$

31. If an ordinary dry cell delivers 30 amp when shortcircuited, which one of the following is the internal resistance of the cell, in ohms?

    A. 0.033 B. 0.05 C. 0.066 D. 0.2

32. When a 60-watt, 120-volt incandescent lamp is connected in parallel with a 40-watt, 120-volt lamp, the combined resistance of the lamps, in ohms, is CLOSEST to which one of the following?

    A. 24 B. 144 C. 240 D. 360

33. The name plate on a certain motor gives the following information: 5hp, 230V, 18 amp,1200 rpm.
    The efficiency of the motor should, therefore, be

    A. 80% B. 85% C. 90% D. 95%

34. In an AC series circuit, there is an inductive reactance of 20 ohms, a capacitive reactance of 10 ohms, and a resistance of 5 ohms.
    The impedance to current flow, in ohms, in this circuit will be CLOSEST to which one of the following?

    A. 6   B. 11   C. 15   D. 35

35. When an inductance coil of 2.5 henrys is tuned to resonate at 100 cycles/sec, the capacitor should have a magnitude, in microfarads, CLOSEST to which one of the following?

    A. 0.5   B. 1.0   C. 10.0   D. 100.0

36. When a resistor, a coil, and a capacitor are connected in series to an AC generator, the current through the capacitor must be in phase with the voltage across the

    A. resistor   B. coil
    C. capacitor   D. whole circuit

37. If two adjacent parallel conductors free to move are placed within 1 cm of each other, and a 20 ampere direct current is sent through each in the same direction, the tendency of the conductors will be to

    A. move apart
    B. remain stationary
    C. come together
    D. rotate in either a clockwise or counter-clockwise direction

38. An electron beam is moving from left to right in a cathode ray tube.
    When a strong S pole is placed above the beam, the electron beam will be deflected

    A. toward the observer   B. vertically upward
    C. away from the observer   D. vertically downward

39. When a pear-shaped metallic shell is charged positively, the potential of the more pointed end is

    A. less than that of the opposite end
    B. greater than that of the opposite end
    C. the same as that of the opposite end
    D. less than that of the adjacent surface

40. When a parallel-plate capacitor is kept connected to a battery of constant emf, and the plates of the capacitor are moved further apart by the use of insulated handles, which one of the following occurs?
    The

    A. capacitance increases
    B. capacitance remains the same
    C. charge on the capacitor remains the same
    D. charge on the capacitor decreases

41. Voltage may be correctly expressed in which one of the following ways?

    A. Coulombs/elementary charge
    B. Coulombs/sec

C. Dynes/cm
D. Joules/elementary charge

42. In the half-wave power supply, the filter capacitor does which one of the following? 42.____
It

    A. increases input voltage variation
    B. increases maximum voltage output
    C. reduces output voltage variation
    D. limits the input voltage

43. The term *effective current,* as used in sinusoidal AC circuits, means the SAME as the 43.____
term _____ current.

    A. average   B. root-mean-square
    C. peak   D. instantaneous

44. When an AC generator produces its peak voltage of 160V, the instantaneous current 44.____
flow, in amperes, in a 20 ohm resistance connected to it will be

    A. 4   B. 5.7   C. 8   D. 28.2

45. Of the following, the material with the HIGHEST resistivity is 45.____

    A. silver   B. copper   C. aluminum   D. nichrome

46. A 0-10 milliampere meter has a resistance of 20 ohms. 46.____
To convert this meter to an ammeter with a range of 0-1 ampere, we should connect a
resistance of

    A. approximately 2000 ohms in series
    B. approximately 2000 ohms in parallel
    C. 200 ohms in series
    D. 1/5 ohm in parallel

47. A 60 watt lamp and a 600 watt toaster are operating in parallel on a 120 volt circuit. 47.____
The resistance ratio of lamp to toaster is

    A. 1/100   B. 1/10   C. 10/1   D. 100/1

48. When the secondary circuit of a transformer is completed, the current in the primary 48.____

    A. decreases
    B. remains the same
    C. increases
    D. increases or decreases, depending on the ratio of turns

49. The phase angle in an alternating current circuit is zero degrees when the circuit 49.____

    A. contains resistance *only*
    B. contains inductance *only*
    C. contains capacitance *only*
    D. is not closed

50. When a capacitor of 10 microfarads capacity is connected to a 100 volt current source, the charge acquired by the capacitor will have a magnitude, in coulombs, of

    A. 10^{-6} B. 10^{-4} C. 10^{2} D. 10^{3}

50.____

KEY (CORRECT ANSWERS)

1. D	11. A	21. B	31. B	41. D
2. C	12. A	22. C	32. B	42. C
3. B	13. D	23. A	33. C	43. B
4. B	14. A	24. B	34. B	44. C
5. D	15. D	25. D	35. B	45. D
6. C	16. A	26. C	36. A	46. D
7. D	17. A	27. B	37. C	47. C
8. B	18. C	28. A	38. C	48. C
9. D	19. D	29. C	39. C	49. A
10. C	20. B	30. B	40. D	50. B

EXAMINATION SECTION

TEST 1

DIRECTIONS: Each question or incomplete statement is followed by several suggested answers or completions. Select the one that BEST answers the question or completes the statement. *PRINT THE LETTER OF THE CORRECT ANSWER IN THE SPACE AT THE RIGHT.*

1. The length of a Marconi-type antenna is _____ wavelength.
    A. ¼   B. ½   C. ¾   D. 1

2. A whip antenna of less than ¼ wavelength will present an electrical impedance that is
    A. resistive
    B. capacitive
    C. inductive
    D. 180° out-of-phase

3. Frequency multiplication is achieved in transmitter stages by operating them as Class _____ amplifiers.
    A. A   B. AB   C. B   D. C

4. The power factor of a resonant circuit is
    A. lagging   B. leading   C. unity   D. zero

5. The power factor of a *parallel* circuit consisting of a 51-ohm resistor and a 51-ohm capacitive reactance is
    A. .500   B. .667   C. .707   D. .887

6. A tunable *series* RLC circuit will have MINIMUM impedance when the
    A. capacitive reactance equals the inductive reactance
    B. inductive reactance or capacitive reactance equals zero
    C. capacitive reactance equals the resistance
    D. inductive reactance equals the resistance

7. At resonance, a tunable *parallel* RLC circuit will be characterized by
    A. broadest bandwidth
    B. lowest "Q"
    C. maximum impedance
    D. equal currents through the resistance, inductance, and capacitance

8. If the number of turns of an inductor is halved, the value of the inductance is
    A. doubled
    B. unchanged
    C. reduced to one-half
    D. reduced to one-quarter

9. The resistivity of copper is GREATER than that of the element
    A. silicon   B. germanium   C. silver   D. gold

2 (#1)

10. The MINIMUM number of 10-microfarad, 25-volt capacitors that can be connected up to yield an equivalent capacitance of 5 microfarads, usable on 150 volts, is
    A. 2   B. 6   C. 18   D. 24

10.____

11. The number of DB's (decibels) corresponding to a power ratio of 200 is MOST NEARLY _____ DB's.
    A. 20   B. 23   C. 26   D. 40

11.____

12. The MAXIMUM current carrying capacity, in amperes, of a resistor marked "5,000 ohms, 200 watts" is
    A. 1/25   B. 1/5   C. 5   D. 25

12.____

13. The combined equivalent resistance of a 12-ohm resistor, a 6-ohm resistor, and a 4-ohm resistor connected in *parallel* is
    A. ½ ohm   B. 1 ohm   C. 2 ohms   D. 3 ohms

13.____

14. The percentage regulation of a power supply with a no-load voltage output of +25.3 volts and a full-load voltage output of +23.0 volts is
    A. 1.9%   B. 2.1%   C. 9%   D. 10%

14.____

15. A capacitance of .0015 microfarads is equal to
    A. 150 picofarads   B. 1500 picofarads
    C. 150 nanofarads   D. 1500 nanofarads

15.____

16. A diode is color coded with a purple, a green, and a red ring in that order (the purple ring is at the end of the diode). It should be concluded from the coding that the diode is a
    A. IN752   B. IN7500   C. IN75B   D. IN7511

16.____

17. The time constant of a resistance and an inductance in *series* can be increased by
    A. *increasing* either the resistance or the inductance
    B. *increasing* the resistance or decreasing the inductance
    C. *decreasing* the resistance or increasing the inductance
    D. *decreasing* either the resistance or the inductance

17.____

18. The combined equivalent impedance of a 50-ohm inductive reactance connected in *parallel* with a 25-ohm capacitive reactance is
    A. 75 ohms inductive reactance   B. 75 ohms capacitive reactance
    C. 50 ohms inductive reactance   D. 50 ohms capacitive reactance

18.____

19. The tree connections of an SCR are the
    A. collector, emitter, and gate   B. base 1, base 2, and emitter
    C. anode, cathode, and gate   D. emitter 1, emitter 2, and base

19.____

20. FET is the abbreviation for a _____ transistor.
    A. fast epitaxial   B. field effect
    C. frequency extended   D. forward emitting

20.____

21. The resonant frequency of a .1 henry inductance and a .001 microfarad capacitance "tank" circuit is MOST NEARLY
    A. 160 Hz   B. 1600 Hz   C. 16 KHz   D. 16 MHz

22. At 300 MHz, electromagnetic energy in air has a wavelength of
    A. 1 centimeter
    B. 10 centimeters
    C. 100 centimeters
    D. 1000 centimeters

23. The frequency range from 300 MHz to 3000 MHz is designated by RETMA and ASA as the _____ range.
    A. HF   B. VHF   C. UHF   D. SHF

24. A modulated carrier wave has a maximum magnitude of 150 volts and 50% modulation.
    If the modulation is removed, the carrier will have a magnitude of _____ volts.
    A. 50   B. 75   C. 100   D. 150

25. If 50 microamperes produces a full-scale deflection on a DC voltmeter, the sensitivity of the instrument is _____ ohms/volt.
    A. 5,000   B. 10,000   C. 20,000   D. 50,000

26. A "beat-frequency meter" is also called a
    A. frequency synthesizer
    B. distortion meter
    C. wave analyzer
    D. heterodyne-frequency meter

27. Assume that a voltmeter uses the same scale for three ranges, 0-300 volts, 0-75 volts, and 0-15 volts.
    If the scale is marked only for the 0-300 volt range, then a scale reading of 120 when the 0-75 volt range is being used will correspond to an ACTUAL voltage of _____ volts.
    A. 10   B. 12   C. 24   D. 30

28. Variations in the signals introduced in the "Z" axis input of an oscilloscope produce corresponding changes in the
    A. positioning of the time-delayed sweep
    B. intensity of the trace
    C. "Y" axis frequency response
    D. "X" axis sawtooth repetition rate

29. When using an ohmmeter to measure resistance, the GREATEST accuracy is obtained when the range selected results in a deflection that is APPROXIMATELY
    A. ¼ full-scale
    B. ½ full-scale
    C. ¾ full-scale
    D. full-scale

30. A grid-dip meter is GENERALLY used to measure
    A. Q   B. modulation   C. RF current   D. frequency

31. A 0-150 volt voltmeter has an accuracy of 2% F.S.
When the pointer shows 75 volts, the MAXIMUM error is plus or minus
   A. .5 volt   B. 1.5 volts   C. 2.0 volts   D. 3.0 volts

31.____

32. Certain attenuation probes used with oscilloscopes provide for an adjustment to be made in each probe, prior to its use. The adjustment is required in order to _____ on which it is used.
   A. match the probe to the circuitry
   B. match the probe to the input of the scope
   C. adjust the DC volts/division sensitivity of the input to the scope
   D. adjust the DC balance of the input to the scope

32.____

33. When an oscilloscope is set up to display a lissajous pattern, the feature that is inhibited and NOT available is the
   A. "Y" axis manual positioning control
   B. "X" axis manual positioning control
   C. automatic retrace blanking
   D. trace intensity manual control

33.____

34. In order to minimize multiple reflections in a coaxial line, the MOST effective steps that should be taken are to drive the sending end with a
   A. low impedance source and terminate the receiving end with a resistance equal to the coaxial characteristic impedance
   B. source with output impedance equal to the coaxial characteristic impedance and terminate the receiving end with a resistance equal to the coaxial characteristic impedance
   C. low impedance source and terminate the receiving end with a high impedance
   D. source with output impedance to the coaxial characteristic impedance and terminate the receiving end with a high impedance

34.____

35. Of the following statements concerning a dual-trace oscilloscope, the one which is CORRECT is that it
   A. requires a two-gun cathode-ray tube
   B. has two "Y" axis inputs that are chopped and displayed as a single trace
   C. uses a single time base when used in the "chopped" mode
   D. uses dual-time bases when used in the "chopped" mode

35.____

36. The type of display usually produced on oscilloscopes, where signal amplitude is convert4ed to a "Y" axis displacement and a time base is introduced on the "X" axis, is CLOSEST in appearance to the radar indicator that is called a(n) _____ scan.
   A. A   B. B   C. J   D. PPI

36.____

37. Of the following, the BEST instrument for measuring very low resistances is the _____ bridge.
   A. Wien   B. Kelvin   C. Hay   D. Maxwell

37.____

38. Of the following, the instrument that should be used in measuring radiation patterns produced by antennas is the
    A. spectrum analyzer
    B. field-strength meter
    C. curve tracer
    D. distortion meter

    38._____

39. Taut-band suspension is a feature which is incorporated in
    A. the internal supporting of hermetic-sealed units
    B. low-friction meter movements
    C. dial cord assemblies
    D. vibration mounts for electronic packages

    39._____

40. A "bolometer" is a device that can be used for measuring
    A. microwave power
    B. static charge
    C. magnetic-field strength
    D. vibration frequencies

    40._____

KEY (CORRECT ANSWERS)

1.	A	11.	B	21.	C	31.	D
2.	B	12.	B	22.	C	32.	B
3.	D	13.	C	23.	C	33.	C
4.	C	14.	D	24.	C	34.	B
5.	C	15.	B	25.	C	35.	C
6.	A	16.	A	26.	D	36.	A
7.	C	17.	C	27.	D	37.	B
8.	D	18.	D	28.	B	38.	B
9.	C	19.	C	29.	B	39.	B
10.	C	20.	B	30.	D	40.	A

TEST 2

DIRECTIONS: Each question or incomplete statement is followed by several suggested answers or completions. Select the one that BEST answers the question or completes the statement. *PRINT THE LETTER OF THE CORRECT ANSWER IN THE SPACE AT THE RIGHT.*

1. One of the reasons why radiotelephones are operated in the 30 MHz to 3000 MHz range is that
    A. skip transmission is very effective
    B. antenna orientation is not important
    C. the number of voice channels is great
    D. AM operation is less noisy than FM

1.____

2. The transmission of a distress message by a radiotelephone station not itself in distress should include calling out three times the expression
    A. SOS   B. SOS relay   C. Mayday   D. Mayday relay

2.____

3. In specifying the characteristics of an oscillator crystal, the information that should be given, together with the frequency tolerance, is the crystal
    A. age
    B. operating temperature range
    C. manufacturer
    D. power supply voltages

3.____

4. Records indicate that a component in a certain unit has been replaced repeatedly, and no such history exists in other similar units with the same type of service and total operation time.
   Based on this information, it should be concluded that
    A. the replacement components were defective
    B. the component was replaced at times when it had not failed
    C. the replacement components were connected into the circuit improperly
    D. there is something else wrong in the unit causing the component to fail

4.____

5. When trouble-shooting a large electronic unit, such as a console, first, power should be removed and the NEXT step should be that
    A. internal capacitors be discharged by using a shorting connection to chassis
    B. ohmmeter checks be made according to the instruction manual
    C. the operating personnel be notified that the unit is out of operation
    D. the door and panel interlocks be by-passed

5.____

6. Metal enclosures and panels of electronic or electrical equipment should be well grounded in order to
    A. protect operating personnel from getting electric shocks
    B. insure that the contained equipment has a good reference ground
    C. prevent static charges from building up on the frame
    D. provide a solid mounting for the equipment and keep it firmly in place

6.____

7. The main reason for NOT using carbon tetrachloride as a cleaning agent on electrical equipment is that it
   A. is an electrical conductor
   B. is too expensive
   C. generates toxic fumes
   D. coats equipment with an acid deposit

8. The MOST likely cause of damage occurring in transistorized circuitry during the process of soldering is due to the application of too much
   A. pressure   B. heat   C. solder   D. rosin flux

9. A 2-inch diameter hole can be made quickly and cleanly in a 16-gauge aluminum plate by the use of a
   A. rat-tail file
   B. nibbler
   C. chassis punch
   D. jig saw

10. A reason for using teflon insulation rather than vinyl on electrical wiring is that teflon is
    A. better for bonding
    B. more flexible
    C. less expensive
    D. more resistant to heat

11. Of the following statements concerning epoxy glue, the one which is CORRECT is that it
    A. dissolves quickly upon contact with water
    B. is prepared from two components that are mixed together shortly before use
    C. is a long-time favorite for making temporary bonds
    D. generally does not require clamps, nails or presses on surfaces to be joined

12. Of the following chemicals, the one which will burn on contact with a lighted match is
    A. carbon tetrachloride
    B. acetone
    C. methylene chloride
    D. sodium bicarbonate

13. Of the following, the BEST method of disposing of spray cans that contain aerosol paints or solvents is
    A. puncturing the cans and then throwing them into an incinerator
    B. puncturing the cans and then having them picked up by the sanitation men
    C. throwing them into an incinerator
    D. having them picked up by the sanitation men

14. An ohmmeter of known polarity is connected from the base to the emitter on a transistor in such manner that the positive lead is on the base. The ohmmeter registers continuity with such conditions and then registers an "open" circuit when the leads are reversed.
    Based on this information, it should be concluded that the transistor is
    A. good   B. defective   C. an NPN   D. a PNP

3 (#2)

15. An ohmmeter registers "open" when connected from the emitter to the collector of a transistor (base left disconnected) and also registers "open" when the leads are reversed. This information suggests that the transistor is
    A. possibly good
    B. definitely defective
    C. an NPN
    D. a PNP

16. In order to get good indications when checking a transistor by using an ohmmeter, yet not cause damage, the voltage across the test leads should _____ 1.5 volts DC and the ohmmeter scale _____ be less than R × 100.
    A. *exceed*; should
    B. *exceed*; should not
    C. *not exceed*; should
    D. *not* exceed; should not

17. If an audio amplifier requiring a 3200-ohm load is connected to the primary winding of a 20:1 step-down output transformer, the matching speaker to be connected to the secondary winding should have an impedance of _____ ohms.
    A. 4
    B. 8
    C. 16
    D. 32

18. The converter stage in a typical heterodyne receiver combines the functions of a(n)
    A. RF stage and the local oscillator
    B. mixer stage and the local oscillator
    C. RF stage and an IF stage
    D. mixer stage and an IF stage

19. One of the reasons why RF stages improve the performance of a typical heterodyne receiver is that they
    A. increase the sensitivity and broaden the bandwidth
    B. provide regenerative action and improve selectivity
    C. increase sensitivity and improve AVC action
    D. improve AVC action and broaden bandwidth

20. Of the following statements concerning the record heads in typical magnetic-tape recorders, the one which is CORRECT is that they are
    A. self-cleaning and require occasional realignment
    B. automatically demagnetized by the signals in the tape-erase heads
    C. easily magnetized and should not be checked for continuity with an ohmmeter
    D. not self-cleaning and are demagnetized by over-driving the record amplifiers

21. Typical recording speeds on commercial magnetic-tape recorders are
    A. 3½ ips, 7 ips, 15 ips, and 30 ips
    B. 3¾ ips, 7 ½ ips, 15 ips, and 30 ips
    C. 3¾ ips, 7 ips, 15 ips, and 25 ips
    D. 3½ ips, 7½ ips, 15 ips, and 30 ips

4 (#2)

22. According to FCC regulations, the frequency and deviation of a crystal-controlled FM transmitter must be checked BEFORE it is put into operation, and rechecked thereafter every
    A. month   B. 3 months   C. 6 months   D. year

22.____

23. According to FCC regulations, radio transmitters may be tuned or adjusted only by persons possessing a
    A. first or second class commercial radiotelephone operator's license
    B. first class commercial radiotelephone operator's license
    C. first or second class commercial radiotelephone operator's license or by personnel working under their immediate supervision
    D. first class commercial radiotelephone operator's license or by personnel working under their immediate supervision

23.____

24. According to FCC regulations, transmitters whose oscillators are not crystal controlled should have their carrier frequencies checked BEFORE they are put into operation, and rechecked thereafter every
    A. week   B. month   C. 3 months   D. 6 months

24.____

25. The FCC dictates that the power in the output stage(s) of a 5-watt transmitter, whose modulation and power setting remain unaltered, should be checked at the time it is put into operation, and rechecked thereafter every
    A. month   B. 3 months   C. 6 months   D. year

25.____

Questions 26-40.

DIRECTIONS: Questions 26 through 40 are to be answered on the basis of the schematic diagram appearing on pages 7 (#2) and 8 (#2).

26. The circuits shown on the schematic represent the stages of a(n)
    A. transmitter   B. receiver
    C. audio-intercom   D. pulse-generator

26.____

27. The types of transistors shown on the schematic are
    A. all NPN's
    B. all PNP's
    C. some NPN's and some PNP's
    D. interchangeable and usable as either NPN's or PNP's

27.____

28. The power supply shown on the schematic supplies the stages with
    A. one B+ voltage, common to all stages
    B. two B+ voltages
    C. one B+ voltage and one B- voltage
    D. two B- voltages

28.____

29. The circuit element designated as Y101, in Oscillator F1 is a
    A. remote-bias adjustment   B. compensated-crystal assembly
    C. solid-stage switching device D. protective interlock

29.____

5 (#2)

30. If the unmodulated frequency at the collector of Q107, of the Final Amplifier, is 135 MHz, then the input frequency to the base of transistor Q103, in the Modulator is _____ MHz.
    A. 3.75   B. 7.50   C. 15.0   D. 22.5

    30._____

31. The component in the Automatic Drive Limiter that has the designation RT101,10K is a
    A. high-resistance incandescent lamp
    B. thermistor
    C. precision wire-wound resistor
    D. ballast lamp

    31._____

32. The component in the power supply that has the designation of CR103 is a
    A. double-anode clipper   B. tunnel diode
    C. zener diode   D. rectifier bridge

    32._____

33. The transistor-stage configuration in which transistor 0109 of the Integrator is connected is called a(n) _____ connection.
    A. emitter-follower   B. phase-splitter
    C. Darlington   D. common-base

    33._____

34. The component between the Amplifier-Clipper and the Integrator that has the designation L116,0.8H is a(n)
    A. air-core choke   B. iron-core inductor
    C. ferrite inductor   D. saturable-core inductor

    34._____

35. Trouble has developed in a unit whose schematic is the one accompanying this test. DC measurements are taken and indicate that the voltage on the base of Q109 in the Integrator stage has gone to -5.6 volts and the emitter voltage has gone to 0.0 volts.
    Of the following, the condition that causes such voltage levels is
    A. the R128 potentiometer slider-arm is making poor contact
    B. Q109 has developed an "open" between base and emitter
    C. C153 has become shorted
    D. Q108, in the previous stage, has gone to cut-off

    35._____

36. If, in the Pre-Amplifier stage shown in the schematic pacitor C164 were to short, the result would be that
    A. Q110 would go harder into conduction
    B. Q110 would approach cut-off
    C. Q110 would become damaged
    D. C165 would break down in the reverse direction

    36._____

37. In the power supply section, capacitor C156 is required in shunt with C155 because
    A. the circuit requires a capacity of slightly more than 15 microfarads; hence, C256 would supply the additional amount
    B. C155 regulates the DC voltage while C156 shunts out ripple frequencies

    37._____

C. C155 is effective in filtering low frequencies, and C156 is effective in filtering high frequencies
D. C155 and C156, in parallel, form a "pi" section of the filter network

38. R113 and C124 in the collector circuit of Q104 in the second Tripler stage form what is COMMONLY called a _____ network.   38._____
    A. self-bias   B. low-frequency peaking
    C. parasitic-suppressor   D. decoupling

39. The Z101 sub-miniature harmonic filter, at the output of the Final Amplifier, is a _____ filter   39._____
    A. lo-pass   B. hi-pass   C. notch   D. bandpass

40. The purpose of C101, in Oscillator F1, is to   40._____
    A. adjust the bias level of the stage
    B. slightly "pull" the frequency of oscillation
    C. tune out the inductance seen looking into the transistor base
    D. suppress parasitic oscillations

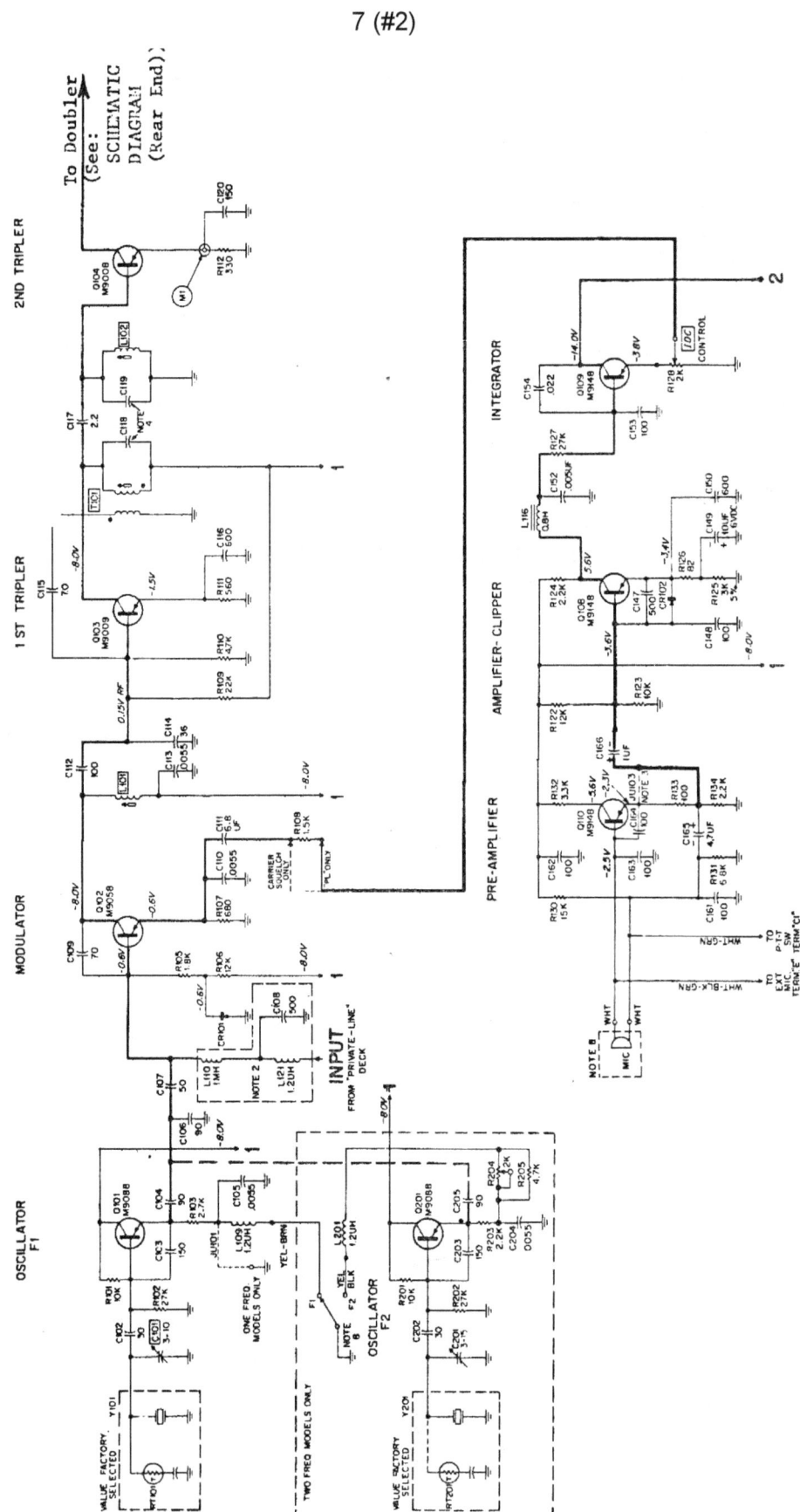

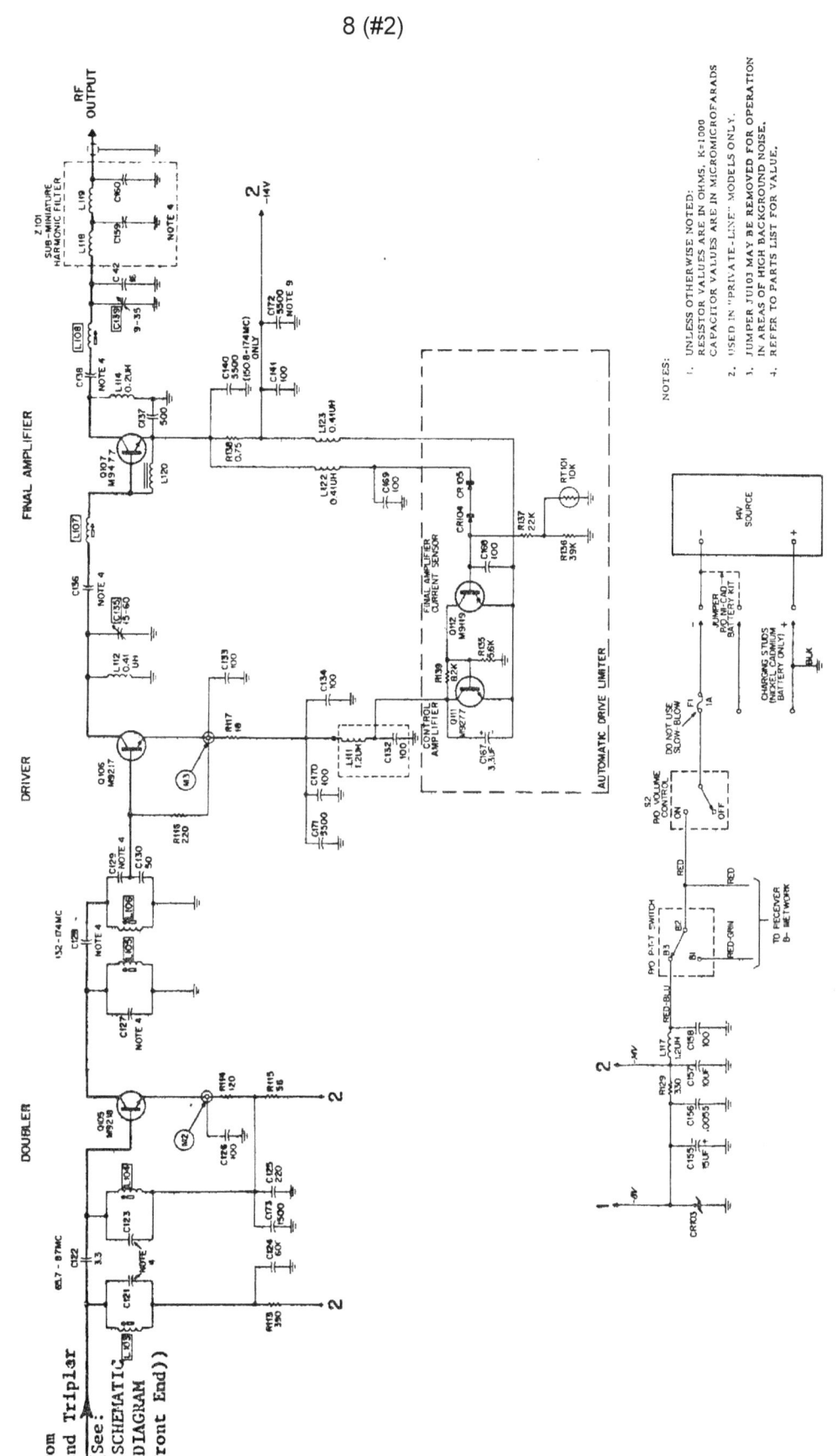

KEY (CORRECT ANSWERS)

1.	C	11.	B	21.	B	31.	B
2.	D	12.	B	22.	D	32.	C
3.	B	13.	D	23.	C	33.	A
4.	D	14.	C	24.	B	34.	B
5.	A	15.	A	25.	D	35.	B
6.	A	16.	D	26.	A	36.	B
7.	C	17.	B	27.	C	37.	C
8.	B	18.	B	28.	D	38.	D
9.	C	19.	C	29.	B	39.	A
10.	D	20.	C	30.	B	40.	B

TEST 3

DIRECTIONS: Each question or incomplete statement is followed by several suggested answers or completions. Select the one that BEST answers the question or completes the statement. *PRINT THE LETTER OF THE CORRECT ANSWER IN THE SPACE AT THE RIGHT.*

1. If an amplifier has three stages each having a gain of ten, the overall gain of the amplifier is 1.____
   A. 30 B. 300 C. 1,000 D. 1,000,000

2. An amplitude-modulated carrier is said to be overmodulated when the 2.____
   A. carrier amplitude sometimes is zero for an appreciable time
   B. audio frequencies exceed the assigned bandwidth
   C. audio frequencies are close to the carrier frequency
   D. carrier amplitude sometimes exceeds the rated tank voltage

3. For a radio receiver in which the tuning is done with variable air condensers, the practical ratio of highest to lowest frequency that can be tuned with a single coil for each condenser is NEAREST to 3.____
   A. 1.5:1 B. 3:1 C. 6:1 D. 12:1

4. A 2k-ohm, a 4k-ohm, a 6k-ohm, and an 8k-ohm resistor are connected in parallel to a 100-volt power source. The resistor which must have the HIGHEST rating, in watts, is the 4.____
   A. 2k-ohm B. 4k-ohm C. 6k-ohm D. 8k-ohm

5. A large number of 10-microfarad, 25-volt condensers are available in a particular laboratory. The MINIMUM number of these required to yield a capacitance of 5 microfarads for operation on 150 volts is 5.____
   A. 2 B. 6 C. 18 D. 24

6. The heaters of three vacuum tubes are to be operated in series with a resistor on a 120-volt circuit. 6.____
   If the ratings of the heaters are respectively 50, 35, and 12 volts, all at 0.15 amp, the MINIMUM rating of the resistor should be
   A. 250 ohms; 5 watts   B. 250 ohms, 10 watts
   C. 150 ohms, 10 watts   D. 150 ohms, 5 watts

7. An audio amplifier is stated to have a frequency response of ±3 db from 50 to 10,000 cps. If the response is down 3 db at 50 cycles, the voltage output at this frequency (50 cycles) compared to the average voltage output throughout the frequency range is ABOUT 7.____
   A. 50% B. 63% C. 67% d. 70%

8. The MAXIMUM limits of resistance of a resistor having yellow, green, and orange color bands (reading from left to right) are 8.____
   A. 44,100 – 45,900   B. 42,750 – 47,250
   C. 41,500 – 49,500   D. 36,000 – 54,000

9. A COMMONLY used IF for FM receivers in the 88-108 mc. range is
   A. 455 kc.   B. 456 kc.   C. 10.7 mc.   D. 22.3 mc.

10. Crystal controlled oscillator frequency stability is maintained MOST closely by
    A. feeding the output into a tuned tank circuit
    B. enclosing the crystal in a temperature controlled oven
    C. mounting the crystal in a shock-proof container
    D. obtaining the input from a tuned tank circuit

11. One COMMONLY used dual triode vacuum tube has the designation
    A. 12AU7   B. 12BE6   C. 12SA7   D. 12SQ7

12. The base radiotelephone station used for contacting surface line patrol cars in operation 24 hours per day would be meeting legal requirements if self-identification were made
    A. 24 times a day
    B. every 2 hours
    C. at the end of each transmission
    D. at the beginning of each day

13. The alphabet used in radiotelephone communication is
    A. Morse
    B. international
    C. telephonic
    D. phonetic

14. A d.c. meter which gives full-scale deflection at 50 microamperes has a sensitivity of _____ ohms/volt.
    A. 1,000   B. 5,000   C. 20,000   D. 50,000

15. A certain d.c. meter which gives full-scale deflection at 50 microamperes has a resistance of 250 ohms. When used to measure current, it reads .50 of full-scale with a 2.5-ohm resistor connected across the meter terminals. The measured current, in milliamperes, is NEAREST to
    A. 1.3   B. 2.5   C. 12.5   D. 25.3

16. A certain train to wayside communication system operates at a frequency of 180 mc. This corresponds to a wavelength of
    A. 1667 meters
    B. 166.7 meters
    C. 1667 centimeters
    D. 166.7 centimeters

17. In an FM receiver using vacuum tubes, the tube having the lowest voltage applied to the plate is USUALLY the
    A. mixer   B. IF amplifier   C. limiter   D. AF amplifier

18. A grid-dip meter is GENERALLY used to measure
    A. frequency   B. RF current   C. AF current   D. modulation

19. To obtain a trapezoidal modulation pattern on the oscilloscope, the signal applied to the horizontal deflection plates should be a
    A. square wave
    B. saw-tooth wave
    C. sample of the final tank-circuit voltage
    D. sample of the audio modulating voltage

    19.____

20. To obtain a wave-envelope modulation pattern on the oscilloscope, the signal applied to the horizontal deflection plates should be a
    A. square wave
    B. saw-tooth wave
    C. sample of the audio modulating voltage
    D. sample of the final tank-circuit voltage

    20.____

21. When soldering transistorized circuitry, the transistors are MOST likely to be damaged from the use of too much
    A. solder   B. rosin flux   C. heat   D. pressure

    21.____

Questions 22-28.

DIRECTIONS: Questions 22 through 28 are to be answered on the basis of the following circuit.

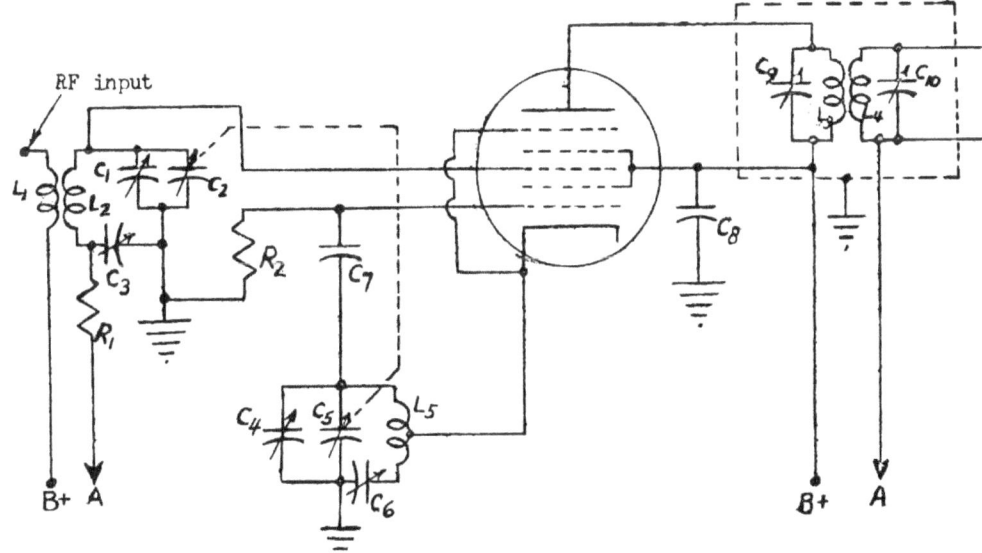

22. The name MOST commonly given to this circuit is
    A. radio-frequency amplifier   B. first detector
    C. intermediate frequency amplifier D. ratio detector

    22.____

23. The vacuum tube shown is a
    A. power amplifier pentode   B. beam power pentode
    C. hexode mixer   D. pentagrid converter

    23.____

24. The wires terminating in arrowheads and labeled A MOST likely connect to the
    A. chassis
    B. AVC bus
    C. cathode bias resistors
    D. power supply screen grid bias

    24.____

25. Tracking at the high-frequency end of the tuning range is synchronized by adjusting
    A. C_1 and C_4
    B. C_3 and C_6
    C. C_2 and C_5
    D. C_3 and C_4

    25.____

26. Tracking at the low-frequency end of the tuning range is synchronized by adjusting
    A. C_1 and C_4
    B. C_3 and C_6
    C. C_2 and C_5
    D. C_3 and C_4

    26.____

27. The circuit shows that there is shielding around the
    A. RF tuning stage
    B. oscillator
    C. vacuum tube
    D. IF transformer

    27.____

28. The type of oscillator shown is a
    A. tickler
    B. Colpitts
    C. Hartley
    D. TPTG

    28.____

29. A 35-ohm, 2-watt, 10% tolerance resistor should have color bands, reading from left to right, of
    A. orange, green, brown, silver
    B. orange, green, brown, gold
    C. orange, green, black, silver
    D. orange, green, black, gold

    29.____

30. The resistor of Question 29 above has a current-carrying capacity of
    A. .239 ma
    B. 2.39 ma
    C. 23.9 ma
    D. 239 ma

    30.____

31. The 20,000 ohms/volt meter having a full-scale deflection of 50 volts reads 45 volts with switch S closed in position 1, and 21 volts when the switch is in position 2 as shown. The value of R is readily calculated to be
    A. .875 megohm
    B. 1.14 megohms
    C. 87,500 ohm
    D. 114,000 ohms

    31.____

32. In the high rejection-ratio trap circuit shown, the device that must be connected between terminals 1 and 2 for proper rejection is a(n)
    A. resistor
    B. RF choke
    C. AF choke
    D. capacitor

    32.____

33. A band elimination filter is MOST accurately illustrated by

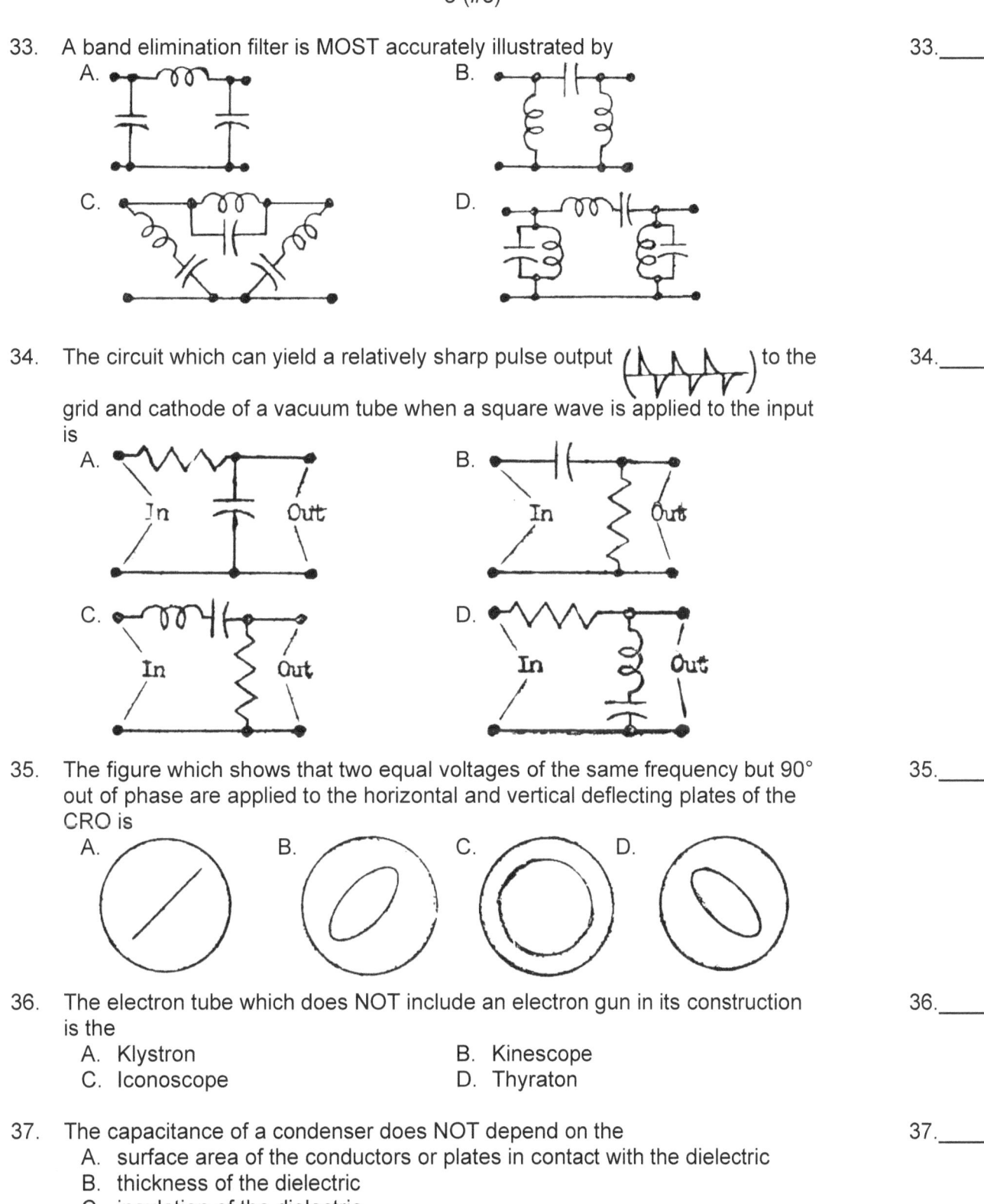

34. The circuit which can yield a relatively sharp pulse output to the grid and cathode of a vacuum tube when a square wave is applied to the input is

35. The figure which shows that two equal voltages of the same frequency but 90° out of phase are applied to the horizontal and vertical deflecting plates of the CRO is

36. The electron tube which does NOT include an electron gun in its construction is the
    A. Klystron
    B. Kinescope
    C. Iconoscope
    D. Thyraton

37. The capacitance of a condenser does NOT depend on the
    A. surface area of the conductors or plates in contact with the dielectric
    B. thickness of the dielectric
    C. insulation of the dielectric
    D. thickness of the plates

38. Frequency doublers and triplers are used in _____ transmitters.
    A. CW   B. pulsed   C. FM   D. keyed

39. Zener diodes are GENERALLY used for
    A. AVC rectification
    B. diode detection
    C. voltage regulation
    D. current limitation

40. An AF amplifier transistor could have the designation
    A. 2N243   B. 242N2   C. 1N105   D. 105N1

41. Carrier frequency voice transmission is used in wire telephony PRIMARILY to increase the
    A. number of voice channels
    B. clarity of tone
    C. transmission distance
    D. transmitted power

42. The circuit shown at the right is PROPERLY called a
    A. potentiometer
    B. voltage divider
    C. voltage decade
    D. current limiter

43. If R_1, R_2, and R_3 in the sketch of Question 42 above are 250k, 500k, and 50k ohms, respectively, the MAXIUM grid bias (negative) voltage available for a tube with a grounded cathode is
    A. 12.5   B. 25   C. 125   D. 250

44. Automobiles now use alternators and rectifiers instead of d.c. generators for supplying the cars' electrical demands. The rectifier that is MOST widely used is the
    A. copper oxide   B. galena   C. germanium   D. silicon

45. A circuit configuration which does NOT apply to transistors is common
    A. emitter   B. base   C. cathode   D. collector

46. The microphone that is MOST likely to require a preamplifier to operate an audio amplifier is the
    A. crystal   B. carbon   C. ceramic   D. magnetic

47. If the oscillator of a tape recorder is faulty, the MOST likely result will be
    A. incomplete erasure
    B. weak recording
    C. excessive volume
    D. variation in tape speed

48. Measurement of radiation from a radio antenna is made with a
    A. Q meter
    B. field strength meter
    C. flux meter
    D. radiometer

49. If a 0-150 volt meter is guaranteed to have an accuracy of 2% of full-scale deflection, then the MAXIMUM error of the indication when the pointer shows 25 volts is plus or minus
    A. 0.5 volt   B. 1.0 volt   C. 1.5 volts   D. 3.0 volts

50. The contacts of relays and switches used in communication work are frequently silver plated. The purpose of the silver plating is to
    A. improve conductivity of the contacts
    B. reduce arcing at the contacts
    C. improve the flexibility of the contacts
    D. reduce the amount of copper that would otherwise be necessary

KEY (CORRECT ANSWERS)

1. C	11. A	21. C	31. B	41. A
2. A	12. C	22. B	32. A	42. B
3. B	13. D	23. D	33. C	43. B
4. A	14. C	24. B	34. B	44. D
5. C	15. B	25. A	35. C	45. C
6. D	16. D	26. B	36. D	46. D
7. D	17. C	27. D	37. D	47. A
8. D	18. A	28. C	38. C	48. B
9. C	19. D	29. C	39. C	49. D
10. B	20. B	30. D	40. A	50. A

TEST 4

DIRECTIONS: Each question or incomplete statement is followed by several suggested answers or completions. Select the one that BEST answers the question or completes the statement. *PRINT THE LETTER OF THE CORRECT ANSWER IN THE SPACE AT THE RIGHT.*

1. If a one microfarad condenser is connected in series with a two microfarad condenser, the capacity of the resulting combination in microfarads is
   A. three
   B. one and one-half
   C. two-thirds
   D. one-third

   1.____

2. A storage battery is charged from a 112-volt d-c line through a series resistance.
   If the charging rate is 10 amperes, the electromotive force of the battery is 12 volts and its internal resistance is 0.2 ohms, the value of the series resistance is _____ ohm.
   A. 11.2   B. 10   C. 9.8   D. 1.2

   2.____

3. The resistance, in ohms, of a 10 ampere 50M.V shunt is MOST NEARLY
   A. 2   B. .05   C. .005   D. .002

   3.____

4. It is required to couple a 4 ohm voice coil of a loudspeaker to an output tube having a plate load of 10,000 ohms. This can best be done by using a transformer having a ratio of primary to secondary turns of APPROXIMATELY
   A. 5   B. 25   C. 50   D. 75

   4.____

5. A dynamoelectric amplifier for power control having high amplification ratio is commonly called a(n)
   A. Dynatron
   B. Amplidyne
   C. Amplitherm
   D. Dynatherm

   5.____

6. An amplifier has an output voltage wave form that does not exactly follow that of the input voltage. This type of distortion is called _____ distortion.
   A. amplitude   B. modular   C. resonance   D. variation

   6.____

7. The frequency in cycles multiplied by 2π is COMMONLY called _____ frequency.
   A. annular   B. heaviside   C. angular   D. circular

   7.____

8. An anion is a negative ion that moves toward the
   A. anode in an electrolytic cell
   B. cathode in a discharge tube
   C. positive terminal of a battery while being discharged
   D. negative terminal of a battery while being charged

   8.____

116

9. Silicon rectifiers, as compared with selenium rectifiers of the same physical size, have
    A. greater current ratings
    B. smaller current ratings
    C. the same current ratings
    D. much greater resistance at 60 cycles

10. The germanium rectifier, as compared with other types of rectifiers, has
    A. a high forward drop
    B. a low reverse resistance
    C. no aging, and therefore has an indefinitely long life
    D. a narrow temperature range, from -5° to +40°C

11. Transistors are ideally suited for Hi-Fi amplifiers since they are inherently _____ devices.
    A. high impedance
    B. low impedance
    C. non-linear
    D. quadrature

12. An air condenser composed of two parallel flat plates of area Z, separated by a distance Y, has a capacitance which is
    A. directly proportional to the distance Y
    B. directly proportional to the area Z
    C. inversely proportional to the area Z
    D. inversely proportional to the square of the area Z

13. For audio frequency amplifiers used for Hi-Fi work, it is desirable to have a hum and noise level, at full output, of APPROXIMATELY _____ db.
    A. -80   B. -20   C. +20   D. +80

14. The maximum Q of cavity resonators is APPROXIMATELY
    A. 500   B. 5,000   C. 50,000   D. 5,000,000

15. To find out if a source of supply is D.C. or A.C., it is BEST to use a(n)
    A. iron vane voltmeter
    B. neon tester
    C. test set made up of two ordinary lamps in series
    D. dynamometer-type voltmeter

16. A vacuum tube circuit having high input impedance, low output impedance, and a gain of less than unit is MOST likely a(n) _____ circuit.
    A. anode-follower
    B. differentiating
    C. ignitron
    D. cathode-follower

17. A heart-shaped pattern obtained as the response or radiation characteristic of certain directional antennae or as the response characteristic of certain microphones is called a
    A. cardioid pattern
    B. sinusoidal pattern
    C. semicircular pattern
    D. parabolic

18. A standard FM broadcast transmitter sends out a signal with a swing of ±60 kc. The percentage modulation of this signal is
    A. 60   B. 70   C. 80   D. 90

19. A standard method of securing a good signal-to-noise ratio in an FM transmitter is to
    A. keep the filament power low to reduce thermal noise
    B. use pre-emphasis
    C. use squelch circuits
    D. use thermal agitation

20. The process of determining the correct values for different positions of a meter, pointer, or settings of a control is COMMONLY called
    A. adjusting   B. measuring   C. aligning   D. calibrating

Questions 21-23.

DIRECTIONS: Questions 21 through 23, inclusive, are to be answered on the basis of the following diagram.

21. In the standard RMA color code for the value of fixed capacitors, when only three color dots are used, the working voltage is assumed to be
    A. 100   B. 300   C. 500   D. 600

22. In standard RMA color code for the value of fixed capacitors when only three color dots are given, the tolerance is assumed to be _____ percent.
    A. 5   B. 10   C. 15   D. 20

23. With reference to the above figure, the dot marked A represents the
    A. first significant figure
    B. decimal multiplier
    C. working temperature
    D. second significant figure

24. If 1000 watts of power are delivered to an antenna having a resistance of 10 ohms, the antenna current, in amperes, is MOST NEARLY
    A. 3.1   B. 5   C. 7.07   D. 10

25. A quarter-wave (90°) antenna comprised of thin wire without supporting structure and operating at a frequency of 5000 kilocycles, has a physical height of _____ feet.
    A. 24.6   B. 49.2   C. 93.8   D. 98.4

26. As compared with the series-fed antenna, the shunt-fed antenna
    A. permits the elimination of the base ground
    B. need not have an impedance match with the source for optimum operation
    C. permits the elimination of the base insulator
    D. permits the elimination of all insulators

27. The above diagram represents a(n)
    A. differentiating circuit
    B. high pass filter
    C. integrating circuit
    D. band pass filter

28. Of the following, the type of bridge used for measuring inductance is the _____ Bridge.
    A. Kelvin   B. Wheatstone   C. Maxwell   D. Newton

29. A certain circuit having an input of one volt and an output of 10 volts has a power gain, in decibels, of
    A. 5   B. 10   C. 15   D. 20

30. In an A.M. transmitter, if the peak value of the modulated carrier current is 2 amps and that of the unmodulated carrier current is one amp, the percentage of modulation is APPROXIMATELY
    A. 40%   B. 60%   C. 80%   D. 100%

31. With reference to vacuum tubes, if the amplification factor is divided by the plate resistance, the result will be a term called
    A. efficiency
    B. transconductance
    C. emission
    D. sensitivity

32. An amplifier in which the grid bias and alternating grid are such that plate current in a specific tube flows at all times with essentially linear amplification is called a class _____ amplifier.
    A. A   B. B   C. C   D. AB$_2$

33. Inverse feedback is used in audio amplifiers to
    A. magnify the amplification
    B. increase the power output
    C. increase the impedance of the loudspeaker
    D. reduce distortion in the output stage

34. Constant-current inverse feedback is USUALLY obtained by
    A. increasing the value of the capacitor across the cathode resistor
    B. omitting the bypass capacitor across the cathode tube
    C. increasing the gain of the output tube
    D. decreasing the plate resistance of the output tube

35. In order to make more natural the reproduction of music which has a very large volume range in a phonograph amplifier, it is BEST to use a(n)
    A. linear response amplifier
    B. volume suppressor
    C. volume expander
    D. output stage with two tubes in push-push

36. The limiter in FM receivers has the function of eliminating _____ from the input to the detector.
    A. the second harmonic
    B. the third harmonic
    C. FM-variations
    D. amplitude variations

Questions 37-39.

DIRECTIONS: Questions 37 through 39 are to be answered on the basis of the following diagram.

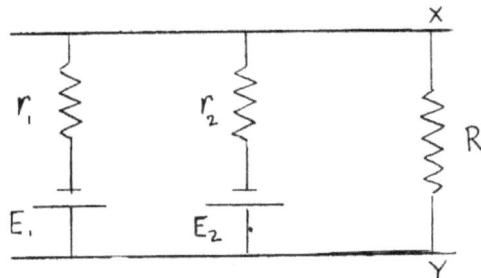

37. If $r_1 = .01$ ohm, $r_2 = .01$ ohm, $E_1 = 1$ volt, and $R = $ infinity, the voltage across xy is MOST NEARLY
    A. 2 volts   B. 1 volt   C. .2 volt   D. .1 volt

38. If $r_1 = .01$ ohm, $r_2 = .01$ ohm, $E_1 = 1$ volt, $E_2 = 2$ volts, and $R = $ infinity, the voltage across xy is MOST NEARLY
    A. .5   B. 1   C. 1.5   D. 2

39. If $r_1 = .01$ ohm, $r_2 = .01$ ohm, $E_1 = 1$ volt, $E_1 = 1$ volt, $E_2 = 2$ volts, and $R = 1$ ohm, the voltage across xy is MOST NEARLY
    A. .5   B. 9   C. 1.1   D. 1.5

40.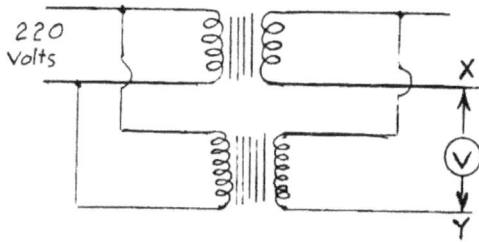

Two transformers with ratios of 2:1 are to be connected in parallel. To test for proper connections, the circuit shown above is used. The transformers may be connected in parallel by connecting Lead "X" to Lead "Y" if the voltmeter shown reads
    A. zero   B. 120   C. 220   D. 340

Questions 41-42.

DIRECTIONS: Questions 41 and 42 are to be answered on the basis of the following figure.

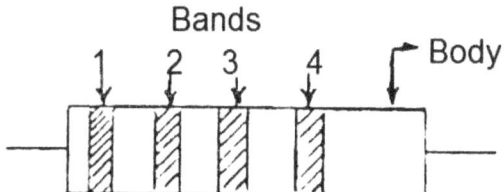

41. In the standard RMA color code chart for the value of resistors, the band numbered 1 in the above figure represents the
    A. decimal multiplier
    B. tolerance
    C. first significant figure
    D. second significant figure

42. With reference to the RMA color code chart for the value of resistors, if the 1st band is red, the 2nd band black, the 3rd band black, and the 4th band silver, the value of this resistor is
    A. 100 ohms 10%
    B. 2000 ohms 5%
    C. 100 ohms 5%
    D. q200 ohms 10%

43. A condenser having a capacitance of one microfarad is connected across a 1000-volt D-C line. The energy stored by this condenser is
    A. 10 watts   B. ½ watt   C. 10 joules   D. ½ joule

44. If a powdered iron core is inserted into an inductance coil, the coil
    A. resistance is increased
    B. inductance is increased
    C. inductance is decreased
    D. resistance is decreased

45. If a brass core is inserted into an inductance coil, the coil
    A. resistance is increased
    B. inductance is increased
    C. inductance is decreased
    D. resistance is decreased

46. A disadvantage of the limiter commonly used in FM receivers is that it requires, for proper operation, a
    A. small signal amplitude
    B. low radio frequency amplification
    C. large signal amplitude
    D. high screen voltage

47. In the ratio detector the radio frequency is fed to the diodes in the same manner as in the FM discriminator except that the diodes in the ratio detector are connected in
    A. parallel   B. push-push   C. push-pull   D. series

48. A general-purpose instrument that may be used for the measurement of the output frequency of an r-f oscillator within accuracies of from .25% to 2% is known as a(n)
    A. absorption wave meter
    B. Wien frequency bridge
    C. Maxwell Bridge
    D. meteorograph bridge

49. The frequency of oscillation of a multivibrator is determined by the values of the
    A. resistance and inductance
    B. inductance and capacity
    C. resistance and capacity
    D. capacity alone

50. With reference to radio-frequency measurements, a primary standard of frequency is defined as one whose frequency is determined
    A. directly in terms of time
    B. by comparison with another standard
    C. by the value of the RC constant
    D. by the values of L and C in the circuit

51. If a .75 kw transmitter produces a field intensity of 10 millivolts per meter at a distance of 5 miles and is received by an antenna having an effective height of 10 meters, the millivolts of signal induced in the antenna (neglecting losses) will be MOST NEARLY
    A. 50   B. 75   C. 100   D. 125

52. With reference to directive microwave antennae, the parabolic reflector possesses the characteristic that
    A. the intensity of the reflected rays varies as the square of the distance
    B. all rays from the radiator striking the reflecting surface are reflected as parallel rays
    C. the intensity of the reflected rays varies inversely as the square of the distance
    D. all rays striking the reflecting surface are reflected as diverging rays

53. With reference to the oscilloscope, Lissajous curves are widely used for
    A. aligning radio I.F. transformers
    B. aligning television tuners
    C. obtaining a response curve of the I.F. stages in FM receivers
    D. frequency comparison

54. The one of the following oscillators which is used to deflect periodically the electron beam of a cathode-ray tube so as to give a displacement that is a function of time is the _____ oscillator.
    A. sweep   B. beat   C. jump   D. connecting

55. The impedance in ohms measured between the terminals of a transmission line at the operating frequency is called _____ impedance.
    A. patch   B. lumped   C. surge   D. sweep

56. Decibels may be calculated by multiplying the common logarithm of the power ratio by ten. Therefore, a power ratio of 100 corresponds to MOST NEARLY
    A. 10 db   B. 20 db   C. 30 db   D. 40 db

57. Power factor is defined as the ratio of active power to apparent power, generally expressed in percent. In accordance with the definition given above, the power factor of a pure resistance is
 A. zero B. unity C. infinity D. indeterminate

Questions 58-59.

DIRECTIONS: Questions 58 and 59 are to be answered on the basis of the following data.

An L resistance attenuation network is required to match, with minimum less, a 500-ohm source Z_S and a 250-ohm lead Z_L; use the design data given below.

$$R_1 = \sqrt{Z_S(Z_S - Z_L)}$$
$$R_2 = \frac{Z_S Z_L}{R_1}$$

58. Using the above data and formula, the value of resistor R_1 for this network is MOST NEARLY
 A. 353 B. 305 C. 253 D. 75

59. With reference to the above L pad and formula, the value of R_2 is MOST NEARLY
 A. 353 B. 305 C. 253 D. 75

60. In frequency modulation receivers, noise
 A. causes an amplitude disturbance only
 B. is completely eliminated by the limiter
 C. causes some variation in the frequency swing of the desired signal
 D. has no effect

61. An open quarter-wave stub may be used as a
 A. suppressor of even and odd harmonics
 B. suppressor of even harmonics only
 C. suppressor of odd harmonics only
 D. filter of odd harmonics only

62. A closed quarter-wave stub offers an infinite impedance at
 A. low frequencies B. high frequencies
 C. the resonant frequency D. all frequencies

63. The one of the following which is COMMONLY used as a standing wave detector operating as a current indicator is a _____ pick-up loop with the ends connected to a _____ galvanometer.
 A. one-turn; r-f thermo B. one-turn; D'Arsonval
 C. 1000-turn; r-f thermo D. 1000-turn; D'Arsonval

64. If a line having a characteristic impedance of 300 ohms is terminated in a resistive load of 50 ohms, the standing-wave ratio is MOST NEARLY
    A. 1 to 12   B. 12 to 1   C. 1 to 6   D. 6 to 1

64.____

65. In aligning the sound discriminator of an FM receiver with an oscilloscope, the pattern that should be obtained for proper adjustment is a(n) _____ curve.
    A. symmetrical "S"   B. asymmetrical "S"
    C. symmetrical parabolic   D. asymmetrical parabolic

65.____

66. In AM radio telephone transmitters, negative feedback
    A. is not used
    B. makes impractical the use of high-efficiency systems
    C. makes impractical the use of a power supply system with relatively inexpensive filtering
    D. decreases the amplitude distortion

66.____

Questions 67-70.

DIRECTIONS: Questions 67 through 70 are to be answered on the basis of the following description of a certain transmitter.

    The radio transmitter is a frequency-modulated unit utilizing the phase-shift method of obtaining frequency deviations, and as such exhibits considerably different characteristics than the usual amplitude-modulated units.

    Intelligence is conveyed in frequency variations of the constant-amplitude carrier wave. The use of the phase-shift method of frequency modulation allows direct crystal control of the mean carrier frequency a necessity in unattended and mobile equipment. It necessitates, however, considerable frequency multiplication after the tubes are used for this function, and a total frequency multiplication of 48 times is effected. A twin triode acts as both crystal oscillator and phase modulator. The first half of the tube operates in a resistance coupled aperiodic oscillator circuit. The output frequency range is 152-162 mc.

    The second half of the twin triode acts as a phase modulator. The r-f output of the crystal oscillator is impressed on the phase-modulator grid by means of a blocking condenser. The cathode circuit is provided with a large amount of degeneration by an unbypassed cathode resistor. Because of this degeneration feedback, the transconductance of the triode is abnormally low—so low that the plate current is affected about as much by the direct grid-plate capacitance as by the transconductance. The two effects result in plate current vectors almost 180° apart, and the total plate current is the resultant of the two components. In phase it will be about 90° removed from the phase of the voltage impressed on the grid. When audio is impressed on the grid thereby periodically changing the bias, and in consequence the transconductance, the plate current undergoes a periodic change in both amplitude and phase. The amplitude modulation is unimportant, and is removed in the frequency multipliers, but the phase modulation remains and is the essential element of the transmitted signal.

67. With reference to the above information, the crystal frequency will be between
    A. 152 and 162 mc   B. 15.2 and 16.2 mc
    C. 3166.67 and 3375.0 Kc   D. 316.67 and 337.50 Kc

67.____

68. In the second part of the twin triode, the cathode resistor 68.____
    A. is shunted by a large condenser
    B. has no condenser
    C. is shunted by a small condenser
    D. is in series with an electrolytic condenser

69. In this transmitter, frequency multiplication occurs 69.____
    A. after modulation   B. before modulation
    C. in the phase modulator   D. in the oscillator circuit

70. With reference to the above information, when the audio is impressed on the 70.____
    grid of the second triode of the twin triode,
    A. the plate current undergoes a change in amplitude only
    B. the plate current undergoes a change in amplitude and phase
    C. any amplitude modulation is cut off by the transconductance
    D. any phase modulation is eliminated.

KEY (CORRECT ANSWERS)

1.	C	11.	B	21.	C	31.	B	41.	C	51.	C	61.	B
2.	C	12.	B	22.	D	32.	A	42.	D	52.	B	62.	C
3.	C	13.	A	23.	A	33.	D	43.	D	53.	D	63.	A
4.	C	14.	C	24.	D	34.	B	44.	B	54.	A	64.	D
5.	B	15.	B	25.	B	35.	C	45.	C	55.	C	65.	A
6.	A	16.	D	26.	C	36.	D	46.	C	56.	B	66.	D
7.	C	17.	A	27.	C	37.	B	47.	D	57.	B	67.	C
8.	A	18.	C	28.	C	38.	C	48.	A	58.	A	68.	B
9.	A	19.	B	29.	D	39.	D	49.	C	59.	A	69.	A
10.	C	20.	D	30.	D	40.	A	50.	A	60.	C	70.	B

TEST 5

DIRECTIONS: Each question or incomplete statement is followed by several suggested answers or completions. Select the one that BEST answers the question or completes the statement. *PRINT THE LETTER OF THE CORRECT ANSWER IN THE SPACE AT THE RIGHT.*

1. The unit of measure of magnetomotive force is the
   A. gilbert   B. gauss   C. henry   D. mho

2. The figure of merit of a coil or circuit is
   A. $\frac{R}{Z}$ B. $\frac{X_L}{R}$ C. $X_c X_L$ D. $Z = R$

3. The molecular friction produced by the alternating current reversals in a magnetic core material is known as
   A. retentivity   B. hysteresis
   C. eddy current   D. counter M.M.F.

4. One horsepower is equal to ____ watts.
   A. 467   B. 647   C. 1646   D. 746

5. The ability of a magnetic material to conduct magnetic lines of force is called
   A. reluctance   B. conductance
   C. permeability   D. admittance

6. A small mica condenser marked with three dots as follows—1. Red, 2. Green, 3. Brown—has a capacitance of what value?
   A. 250 mmf   B. 2500 mmf   C. 25 mmf   D. 2.5 mmf

7. If the current through the windings of an electromagnet is constantly increased, the field strength will increase in proportion to the current, up to a certain point, beyond which the field strength will increase only slightly for a further increase in current. This point is called
   A. permeability   B. saturation
   C. BH curve   D. phase point

8. Gold band on a resistor indicates a tolerance of
   A. 10%   B. 20%   C. 5%   D. 15%

9. Placing a "permeability slug" into an rf transformer will
   A. decrease the frequency of the ckt.
   B. increase the frequency of the ckt.
   C. decrease the inductance
   D. none of the above

10. What law states that the total current entering a junction in a circuit is equal to the total current leaving that junction?
    A. Lenz's   B. Coulomb's   C. Ohm's   D. Kirchhoff's

11. The MAXIMUM current carrying capacity of a resistor marked "5000 Ohms-200 Watts" is _____ amperes.
    A. 25 B. .2 C. 2 D. 2.5

12. Three condensers of 2 uF, 2 uF, and 4 uF are connected in series. The resulting capacitance of this combination will be _____ uF.
    A. 0.8 B. 8.0 C. 1.6 D. 16

13. In order to obtain the maximum short circuit current from a group of similar cells in a storage battery, they should be connected in
    A. parallel
    B. series-parallel
    C. series
    D. parallel-series

14.

   I_T equals _____ amp.
   A. .5 B. 5½ C. 2 D. 0

15. A resistor marked as follows—Body: red; Tip: Green; Band or dot: Orange—has a value of how many ohms?
    A. 1400 ohms
    B. 36,000 ohms
    C. 25,000 ohms
    D. .25 MEG

16. A 10W, 1000 ohm resistor is in parallel with a 100W, 10,000 ohm resistor and a 50W, 20,000 ohm resistor. The HIGHEST permissible line voltage for this combination without exceeding the power ratings of these resistors is
    A. 1,000 volts B. 10 volts C. 100 volts D. 500 volts

17. The fully charged condition of a lead acid storage cell is indicated when a hydrometer reads
    A. 1.080 B. 1.280 C. 1.150 D. 1.500

18. You are called upon to repair, if possible, a storage battery which is discharged and in which the cells are only half full of electrolyte. You should FIRST
    A. fill with a solution of acid and water to 1200 S.G.
    B. fill with plain distilled water and charge
    C. pour out remaining electrolyte and refill with a new solution of water and acid to 1200 S.G.
    D. none of the above—the battery is beyond repair

19. [circuit diagram with battery, R₁, voltmeter, R₂, R₃ in series]

The voltmeter connected as shown above will read the voltage drop across
   A. R_1 B. R_2 C. R_1 and R_2 D. R_2 and R_3

20. A radio receiver has a power transformer designed to supply 250 volts when operating from a 110-volt, 60-cycle supply line.
When the primary is connected to a 110-volt D.C. source, the
   A. secondary voltage will decrease
   B. secondary voltage will increase
   C. primary current will decrease
   D. primary current will increase

21. A coupling system that passes certain frequencies and at the same time rejects other frequencies is called
   A. choke   B. phase shifter
   C. filter   D. bypass condenser

22. Audio frequencies lie between
   A. 200 to 200,000 cps   B. 20 to 20,000 cps
   C. 60 to 120 cps   D. 5 to 4,000 cps

23. Vertical sweep circuits may be distinguished from horizontal by their
   A. higher plate voltages   B. larger capacity condensers
   C. greater power ratings on controls   D. lower plate voltages

24. In an inverted amplifier, output is taken from the _____ circuit.
   A. plate   B. cathode   C. control grid   D. shield grid

25. Poor reception on a newly installed commercial television receiver GENERALLY indicates
   A. improper adjustment of I.F. stages
   B. improper adjustment of 8.25 Mc trap
   C. wrong value R-C components in sweep circuits
   D. poor antenna installation

26. The voltage across the output of the discriminator at resonance should
   A. be a maximum
   B. be a minimum
   C. vary between a maximum and a minimum
   D. be a value depending on the signal voltage

27. For optimum operation of an A.F. resistance coupled voltage amplifier using a triode (not considering frequency restrictions), the plate resistor should be
    A. equal to the plate resistance of the tube
    B. equal to the transconductance of the tube
    C. twice the plate resistance of the tube
    D. equal to plate voltage divided by plate current of the tube

28. Peak inverse voltage being delivered to a full wave rectifier with condenser input is equal to r.m.s. of total secondary
    A. X 1.414
    B. X .707
    C. X. 636
    D. plus voltage on condenser

29. In performing a visual alignment, the voltage fed into the stages to be aligned MUST be
    A. amplitude modulated
    B. unmodulated
    C. frequency modulated
    D. demodulated

30. The discriminator in an FM receiver corresponds to the stage in an AM receiver known as the
    A. converter
    B. second detector
    C. output amplifier
    D. preselector

31. A 200 mmfd padder is connected in series with a 400 mmfd tuning condenser. The total MAXIMUM capacity will be _____ mmfd.
    A. 600   B. 300   C. 133   D. 266

32. Shunting a "tank circuit" with an inducftance will make it
    A. respond to a higher frequency
    B. respond to a lower frequency
    C. destroy its oscillatory action
    D. decrease its resistive component

33. Video frequencies in modern television service range from
    A. 15-15,000 cps
    B. 30-3,500 cps
    C. 44-71 mcs
    D. 4.3-12 mcs

34. A superheterodyne is tuned to a desired signal at 1000 Kc. Its conversion oscillator is operating at 1300 Kc. A signal at _____ Kc may cause an image interference.
    A. 300   B. 900   C. 1600   D. 100

35. The plate E of an RF or IF stage is above normal. The screen grid E is above normal. The cathode E is above normal. Trouble PROBABLY is (E = voltage)
    A. open screen dropping resistor
    B. shorted plate loud resistor
    C. open cathode resistor
    D. shorted screen bi-pass condenser

36. Low output voltage from AC/DC power supply may be caused by open
    A. output filter condenser
    B. condenser in power amplifier cathode circuit
    C. condenser on input side of filter
    D. coupling condenser to power amplifier

37. Adjustments in Lelcher-Wires are GENERALLY accomplished by
    A. sliding a shorting-bar along the line
    B. trimming off the ends of the line
    C. placing a variable condenser across the lines
    D. varying the spacing between the lines

38. Local oscillators in FM receivers often have a mica and a ceramic condenser in parallel across the tank. The purpose of this combination is to
    A. increase the "Q" of the circuit
    B. operate the tank at a greater C/L ratio
    C. prevent temperature co-efficient drift
    D. prevent breakdown of condensers

39. A signal reaching the grid of a grid-leak type of limiter, at a peak value greater than the bias on the tube, will PROBABLY cause
    A. lack of linearity in discriminator output
    B. second-harmonic distortion in A.F. output
    C. saturation in the discriminator "S" curve
    D. normal operation of the stage

40. Frequency adjustments in Klystron tubes are GENERALLY made by
    A. sliding a shorting-bar along the lines
    B. mechanically compressing the tube along its length
    C. tuning the pickup loop
    D. changing the grid-bias

41. The second harmonic of 200 meters is _____ meters.
    A. 400   B. 100   C. 800   D. 50

42. To reduce the natural resonant frequency of a Marconi antenna, we may
    A. place an inductance in series with the antenna
    B. place a condenser in series with the antenna
    C. operate the antenna on a harmonic
    D. reduce the physical length of the antenna

43. The length of a ¼ wave vertical radiator for 800 Kc operation should be ABOUT _____ meters.
    A. 200   B. 94   C. 400   D. 367

44. Alignment of a discriminator is BEST checked by
    A. use of an output meter   B. use of an audio analyzer
    C. use of a vacuum tube voltmeter   D. ear

45. A line may be kept non-resonant by
    A. terminating the line at its natural impedance
    B. keeping it an even number of ¼ waves long
    C. twisting or transposing the wires
    D. running one conductor inside the other

46. Placing a reflector behind a di-pole antenna makes it
    A. non-directional
    B. directional away from the reflector
    C. directional toward the side on which the reflector is placed
    D. directional toward its end

47. Klystron tubes depend for their action upon
    A. parallel-line tanks connected to the grids
    B. class "C" operation with a TPTG circuit
    C. bunching of electrons in a velocity-electron stream
    D. circular rotation of electrons under a strong magnetic influence

48. Ordinary vacuum tubes are ineffective in UHF circuits because
    A. their plate currents are too high
    B. heater voltages of 6.3V a.c. are impractical at ultra-high frequencies
    C. socket terminals will arc over at UHF
    D. inter-electrode capacities are too high for ultra-high frequencies

49. Wave-guides are NOT used at low frequencies because
    A. long waves cannot be guided
    B. power is too great at low frequencies
    C. their physical size would be impractical
    D. the wavelength of low frequencies is too short

50. The hum frequency of a full wave rectifier is _____ the frequency of the line voltage frequency.
    A. once
    B. twice
    C. three times
    D. four times

KEY (CORRECT ANSWERS)

1.	A	11.	B	21.	C	31.	C	41.	B
2.	B	12.	A	22.	B	32.	A	42.	A
3.	B	13.	A	23.	B	33.	B	43.	B
4.	D	14.	B	24.	B	34.	C	44.	C
5.	C	15.	C	25.	D	35.	C	45.	A
6.	A	16.	C	26.	B	36.	C	46.	B
7.	B	17.	B	27.	C	37.	A	47.	C
8.	C	18.	B	28.	A	38.	C	48.	D
9.	A	19.	D	29.	C	39.	D	49.	C
10.	D	20.	D	30.	B	40.	B	50.	B

GLOSSARY OF ELECTRONIC TERMS

TABLE OF CONTENTS

	Page
Acorn Tube ... Bias	1
Biasing Resistor ... Coefficient of Coupling (K)	2
Condenser ... Dielectric	3
Dielectric Constant ... Electrostatic Field	4
Equivalent Circuit ... Henry (h)	5
Helmholts Coil ... Klystron	6
Lag ... Neutralisation	7
Node ... Plate Resistance (r_p)	8
Positive Feedback ... Relaxation Oscillator	9
Reluctance ... Solenoid	10
Space Charge ... Unbalanced Line	11
Unidirectional ... Z	12

ELECTRONICS SYMBOLS

Amplifier ... Cell, Photosensitive	13
Circuit Breaker ... Discontinuity	14
Electron Tube ... Inductor	15
Key, Telegraph ... Meter, Instrument	16
Mode Transducer ... Semiconductor Device	17
Squib ... Transformer	18
Vibrator, Interrupter ... Visual Signaling Device	19

TRANSISTOR SYMBOLS	19
TUBE SYMBOLS	20

GLOSSARY OF ELECTRONIC TERMS

Acorn tube. An acorn-shaped vacuum tube designed for ultra-high-frequency circuits. The tube has short electron transit time and low inter-electrode capacitance because of close spacing and small size electrodes.

Align. To adjust the tuned circuits of a receiver or transmitter for maximum signal response.

Alternation. One-half of a complete cycle.

Ammeter. An instrument for measuring the electron flow in amperes.

Ampere (amp). The basic unit of current or electron flow.

Amplification (A). The process of increasing the strength of a signal.

Amplification factor (ft). The ratio of a small change in plate voltage to a small change in grid voltage, with all other electrode voltages constant, required to produce the same small change in plate current.

Amplifier. A device used to increase the signal voltage, current, or power, generally composed of a vacuum tube and associated circuit called a stage. It may contain several stages in order to obtain a desired gain.

Amplitude. The maximum instantaneous value of an alternating voltage or current, measured in either the positive or negative direction.

Amplitude distortion. The changing of a waveshape so that it is no longer proportional to its original form. Also known as harmonic distortion.

Anode. A positive electrode; the plate of a vacuum tube.

Antenna. A device used to radiate or absorb r-f energy.

Aquadag. A graphite coating on the inside of certain cathode-ray tubes for collecting secondary electrons emitted by the screen.

Array (antenna). An arrangement of antenna elements, usually di-poles, which results in desirable directional characteristics.

Attenuation. The reduction in the strength of a signal.

Audio frequency (a-f). A frequency which can be detected as a sound by the human ear. The range of audio frequencies extends approximately from 20 to 20,000 cycles per second.

Autodyne circuit. A circuit in which the same elements and vacuum tube are used as an oscillator and as a detector. The output has a frequency equal to the difference between the frequencies of the received signal and the oscillator signal.

Automatic gain control (age) A method of automatically regulating the gain of a receiver so that the output tends to remain constant though the incoming signal may vary in strength.

Automatic volume control (avc). See Automatic gain control.

Autotransformer. A transformer in which part of the primary winding is used as a secondary winding, or vice versa.

Azimuth. The angular measurement in a horizontal plane and in a clockwise direction, beginning at a point oriented to north.

Ballast resistance. A self-regulating resistance, usually connected in the primary circuit of a power transformer to compensate for variations in the line voltage.

Ballast tube. A tube which contains a ballast resistance.

Band of frequencies. The frequencies existing between two definite limits.

Band-pass filter. A circuit designed to pass with nearly equal response all currents having frequencies within a definite band, and to reduce substantially the amplitudes of currents of all frequencies outside that band.

Bazooka. See Line-balance converter.

Beam-power tube. A high vacuum tube in which the electron stream is directed in concentrated beams from the cathode to the plate. Variously termed beam-power tetrode and beam-power pentode.

Beat frequency. A frequency resulting from the combination of two different frequencies. It is numerically equal to the difference between or the sum of these two frequencies.

Beat note. See Beat frequency.

Bias. The average d-c voltage maintained between the cathode and control grid of a vacuum tube.

Biasing resistor. A resistor used to provide the voltage drop for a required bias.

Blanking. See Gating.

Bleeder. A resistance connected in parallel with a power-supply output to protect equipment from excessive voltages if the load is removed or substantially reduced; to improve the voltage regulation, and to drain the charge remaining in the filter capacitors when the unit is turned off.

Blocking capacitor. A capacitor used to block the flow of direct current while permitting the flow of alternating current.

Break-down voltage. The voltage at which an insulator or dielectric ruptures, or at which ionization and conduction take place in a gas or vapor.

Brilliance modulation. See Intensity modulation.

Buffer amplifier. An amplifier used to isolate the output of an oscillator from the effects produced by changes in voltage or loading in following circuits.

Buncher. The electrode of a velocity-modulated tube which alters the velocity of electrons in the constant current beam causing the electrons to become bunched in a drift space beyond the buncher electrode.

Bypass capacitor. A capacitor used to provide an alternating current path of comparatively low impedance around a circuit element.

Capacitance. The property of two or more bodies which enables them to store electrical energy in an electrostatic field between the bodies.

Capacitive coupling. A method of transferring energy from one circuit to another by means of a capacitor that is common to both circuits.

Capacitive reactance (X_c). The opposition offered to the flow of an alternating current by capacitance, expressed in ohms.

Capacitor. Two electrodes or sets of electrodes in the form of plates, separated from each other by an insulating material called the dielectric.

Carrier. The r-f component of a transmitted wave upon which an audio signal or other form of intelligence can be impressed.

Catcher. The electrode of a velocity-modulated tube which receives energy from the bunched electrons.

Cathode (K). The electrode in a vacuum tube which is the source of electron emission. Also a negative electrode.

Cathode bias. The method of biasing a tube by placing the biasing resistor in the common cathode return circuit, making the cathode more positive, rather than the grid more negative, with respect to ground.

Cathode follower. A vacuum-tube circuit in which the input signal is applied between the control grid and ground, and the output is taken from the cathode and ground. A cathode follower has a high input impedance and a low output impedance.

Characteristic impedance (Z_0). The ratio of the voltage to the current at every point along a transmission line on which there are no standing waves.

Choke. A coil which impedes the flow of alternating current of a specified frequency range because of its high inductive reactance at that range.

Chopping. See Limiting.

Clamping circuit. A circuit which maintains either amplitude extreme of a waveform at a certain level of potential.

Class A operation. Operation of a vacuum tube so that plate current flows throughout the entire operating cycle and distortion is kept to a minimum.

Class AB operation. Operation of a vacuum tube with grid bias so that the operating point is approximately halfway between Class A and Class B.

Class B operation. Operation of a vacuum tube with bias at or near cut-off so that plate current flows during approximately one-half cycle.

Class C operation. Operation of a vacuum tube with bias considerably beyond cut-off so that plate current flows for less than one-half cycle.

Clipping. See Limiting.

Coaxial cable. A transmission line consisting of two conductors concentric with and insulated from each other.

Coefficient of coupling (K). A numerical indication of the degree of coupling existing between two circuits, expressed in terms of either a decimal or a percentage.

Condenser. See Capacitor.

Conductance (G). The ability of a material to conduct or carry an electric current. It is the reciprocal of the resistance of the material, and is expressed in *ohms*.

Continuous waves. Radio waves which maintain a constant amplitude and a constant frequency.

Control grid (G). The electrode of a vacuum tube other than a diode upon which the signal voltage is impressed in order to control the plate current.

Control-grid-plate transconductance. See Transconductance.

Conversion transconductance (gc). A characteristic associated with the mixer function of vacuum tubes, and used in the same manner as transconductance is used. It is the ratio of the i-f current in the primary of the first i-f transformer to the r-f signal voltage producing it.

Converter. See Mixer.

Converter tube. A multielement vacuum tube used both as a mixer and as an oscillator in a superheterodyne receiver. It creates a local frequency and combines it with an incoming signal to produce an intermediate frequency.

Counting circuit. A circuit which receives uniform pulses representing units to be counted and produces a voltage in proportion to their frequency.

Coupled impedance. The effect produced in the primary winding of a transformer by the influence of the current flowing in the secondary winding.

Coupling. The association of two circuits in such a way that energy may be transferred from one to the other.

Coupling element. The means by which energy is transferred from one circuit to another; the common impedance necessary for coupling.

Critical coupling. The degree of coupling which provides the maximum transfer of energy between two resonant circuits at the resonant frequency.

Crystal (Xtal). (1) A natural substance, such as quartz or tourmaline, which is capable of producing a voltage stress when under pressure, or producing pressure when under an applied voltage. Under stress it has the property of responding only to a given frequency when cut to a given thickness.

(2) A nonlinear element such as gelena or silicon, in which case the piezo-electric characteristic is not exhibited.

Crystal mixer. A device which employs the nonlinear characteristic of a crystal (nonpiezo-electric type) and a point contact to mix two frequencies.

Crystal oscillator. An oscillator circuit in which a piezoelectric crystal is used to control the frequency and to reduce frequency instability to a minimum.

Current (J). Flow of electrons; measured in amperes.

Cut-off (c.o.). The minimum value of negative grid bias which prevents the flow of plate current in a vacuum tube.

Cut-off limiting. Limiting the maximum output voltage of a vacuum-tube circuit by driving the grid beyond cut-off.

Cycle. One complete positive and one complete negative alternation of a current or voltage.

Damped waves. Waves which decrease exponentially in amplitude.

Decoupling network. A network of capacitors and chokes, or resistors, placed in leads which are common to two or more circuits to prevent unwanted interstage coupling.

Deflection sensitivity (CRT). The quotient of the displacement of the electron beam at the place of impact by the change in the deflecting field. It is usually expressed in millimeters per volt applied between the deflection electrodes, or in millimeters per gauss of the deflecting magnetic field.

Degeneration. The process whereby a part of the output signal of an amplifying device is returned to its input circuit in such a manner that it tends to cancel the input.

De-ionization potential. The potential at which ionization of the gas within a gas-filled tube ceases and conduction stops.

Demodulation. See Detection.

Detection. The process of separating the modulation component from the received signal.

Dielectric. An insulator; a term applied to the

insulating material between the plates of a capacitor.

Dielectric constant. The ratio of the capacitance of a capacitor with a dielectric between the electrodes to the capacitance with air between the electrodes.

Differentiating circuit. A circuit which produces an output voltage substantially in proportion to the rate of change of the input voltage.

Diode. A two-electrode vacuum tube containing a cathode and a plate.

Diode detector. A detector circuit employing a diode tube.

Dipole antenna. Two metallic elements, each approximately one quarter wavelength long, which radiate r-f energy fed to them by the transmission line.

Directly heated cathode. A filament cathode which carries its own heating current for electron emission, as distinguished from an indirectly heated cathode.

Director (antenna). A parasitic antenna placed in front of a radiating element so that r-f radiation is aided in the forward direction.

Distortion. The production of an output waveform which is not a true reproduction of the input waveform. Distortion may consist of irregularities in amplitude, frequency, or phase.

Distributed capacitance. The capacitance that exists between the turns in a coil or choke, or between adjacent conductors or circuits, as dis- tinguished from the capacitance which is concentrated in a capacitor.

Distributed inductance. The inductance that exists along the entire length of a conductor, as distinguished from the self-inductance which is concentrated in a coil.

Doorknob tube. A doorknob-shaped vacuum tube designed for ultra-high-frequency circuits. This tube has short electron transit time and low interelectrode capacitance, because of the close spacing and small size of electrodes.

Dropping resistor. A resistor used to decrease a given voltage to a lower value.

Dry electrolytic capacitor. An electrolytic capacitor using a paste instead of a liquid electrolyte. *See* Electrolytic capacitor.

Dynamic characteristics. The relation between the instantaneous plate voltage and plate current of a vacuum tube as the voltage applied to the grid is moved; thus, the characteristics of a vacuum tube during operation.

Dynatron. A negative resistance device; particularly, a tetrode operating on that portion of its i_p vs. e_p characteristic where secondary emission exists to such an extent that an increase in plate voltage actually causes a decrease in plate current, and, therefore, makes the circuit behave like a negative resistance.

Eccles-Jordan circuit (trigger circuit). A direct coupled multivibrator circuit possessing two conditions of stable equilibrium. Also known as a flip-flop circuit.

Effective value. The equivalent heating value of an alternating current or voltage, as compared to a direct current or voltage. It is 0.707 times the peak value of a sine wave. It is also called the rms value.

Efficiency. The ratio of output to input power, generally expressed as a percentage.

Electric field. A space in which an electric charge will experience a force exerted upon it.

Electrode. A terminal at which electricity passes from one medium into another.

Electrolyte. A water solution of a substance which is capable of conducting electricity. An electrolyte may be in the form of either a liquid or a paste.

Electrolytic capacitor. A capacitor employing a metallic plate and an electrolyte as the second plate separated by a dielectric which is produced by electrochemical action.

Electromagnetic field. A space field in which electric and magnetic vectors at right angles to each other travel in a direction at right angles to both.

Electron. The negatively charged particles of matter. The smallest particle of matter.

Electron emission. The liberation of electrons from a bo]difference.

Electronic switch. A circuit which causes a start-and-stop action or a switching action by electronic means.

Electronic voltmeter. *See* Vacuum tube voltmeter.

Electrostatic field. The field of influence

between two charged bodies.

Equivalent circuit. A diagrammatic arrangement of coils, resistors, and capacitors, representing the effects of a more complicated circuit in order to permit easier analysis.

Farad (f). The unit of capacitance.

Feedback. A transfer of energy from the output circuit of a device back to its input.

Field. The space containing electric or magnetic lines of force.

Field intensity. Electrical strength of a field.

Filament. See Directly heated cathode.

Filter. A combination of circuit elements designed to pass a definite range of frequencies, attenuating all others.

Firing potential. The controlled potential at which conduction through a gas-filled tube begins.

First detector. See Mixer.

Fixed bias. A bias voltage of constant value, such as one obtained from a battery, power supply, or generator.

Fixed capacitor. A capacitor which has no provision for varying its capacitance.

Fixed resistor. A resistor which has no provision for varying its resistance.

Fluorescence. The property of emitting light as the immediate result of electronic bombardment.

Fly-back. The portion of the time base during which the spot is returning to the starting point. This is usually not seen on the screen of the cathode-ray tube, because of gating action or the rapidity with which it occurs.

Free electrons. Electrons which are loosely held and consequently tend to move at random among the atoms of the material.

Free oscillations. Oscillatory currents which continue to flow in a tuned circuit after the impressed voltage has been removed. Their frequency is the resonant frequency of the tuned circuit.

Frequency (f). The number of complete cycles per second existing in any form of wave motion; such as the number of cycles per second of an alternating current.

Frequency distortion. Distortion which occurs as a result of failure to amplify or attenuate equally all frequencies present in a complex wave.

Frequency modulation. See Modulation.

Frequency stability. The ability of an oscillator to maintain its operation at a constant frequency.

Full-wave rectifier circuit. A circuit which utilizes both the positive and the negative alternations of an alternating current to produce a direct current.

Gain (A). The ratio of the output power, voltage, or current to the input power, voltage, or current, respectively.

Gas tube. A tube filled with gas at low pressure in order to obtain certain desirable characteristics.

Gating (cathode-ray tube). Applying a rectangular voltage to the grid or cathode of a cathode-ray tube to sensitize it during the sweep time only.

Grid current. Current which flows between the cathode and the grid whenever the grid becomes positive with respect to the cathode.

Grid detection. Detection by rectification in the grid circuit of a detector.

Grid leak. A high resistance connected across the grid capacitor or between the grid and the cathode to provide a d-c path from grid to cathode and to limit the accumulation of charge on the grid.

Grid limiting. Limiting the positive grid voltage (minimum output voltage) of vacuum-tube circuit by means of a large series grid resistor.

Ground. A metallic connection with the earth to establish ground potential. Also, a common return to a point of zero r-f potential, such as the chassis of a receiver or a transmitter.

Half-wave rectification. The process of rectifying an alternating current wherein only one-half of the input cycle is passed and the other half is blocked by the action of the rectifier, thus producing pulsating direct current.

Hard tube. A high vacuum electronic tube.

Harmonic. An integral multiple of a fundamental frequency. (The second harmonic is twice the frequency of the fundamental or first harmonic.)

Harmonic distortion. Amplitude distortion.

Heater. The tube element used to indirectly heat a cathode.

Henry (h). The basic unit of inductance.

Helmholts coil. A variometer having horizontal and vertical balanced coil windings, used to vary the angle of phase difference between any two similar waveforms of the same frequency.

Heterodyne. To beat or mix two signals of different frequencies.

High-frequency resistance. The resistance presented to the flow of high-frequency current. *See* Skin effect.

Horn radiator. Any open-ended metallic device for concentrating energy from a waveguide and directing this energy into space.

Hysteresis. A lagging of the magnetic flux in a magnetic material behind the magnetizing force which is producing it.

Image frequency. An undesired signal capable of beating with the local oscillator signal of a superheterodyne receiver which produces a difference frequency within the bandwidth of the i-f channel.

Impedance (Z). The total opposition offered to the flow of an alternating current. It may consist of any combination of resistance, inductive reactance, and capacitive reactance.

Impedance coil. *See* Choke.

Impedance coupling. The use of a tuned circuit or an impedance coil as the common coupling element between two circuits.

Impulse. Any force acting over a comparatively short period of time, such as a momentary rise in voltage.

Indirectly heated cathode. A cathode which is brought to the temperature necessary for electron emission by a separate heater element. Compare *Directly heated cathode.*

Inductance (L). The property of a circuit which tends to oppose a change in the existing current.

Induction. The act or process of producing voltage by the relative motion of a magnetic field across a conductor.

Inductive reactance (X_1). The opposition to the flow of alternating or pulsating current caused by the inductance of a circuit. It is measured in ohms.

Inductor. A circuit element designed so that its inductance is its most important electrical property; a coil.

Infinite. Extending indefinitely; having innumerable parts, capable of endless division within itself.

In phase. Applied to the condition that exists when two waves of the same frequency pass through their maximum and minimum values of like polarity at the same instant.

Instantaneous value. The magnitude at any particular instant when a value is continually varying with respect to time.

Integrating circuit. A circuit which produces an output voltage substantially in proportion to the frequency and amplitude of the input voltage.

Intensify. To increase the brilliance of an image on the screen of a cathode-ray tube.

Intensity modulation. The control of the brilliance of the trace on the screen of a cathode-ray tube in conformity with the signal.

Interelectrode capacitance. The capacitance existing between the electrodes in a vacuum tube.

Intermediate frequency (i-f). The fixed frequency to which r-f carrier waves are converted in a superheterodyne receiver.

Inverse peak voltage. The highest instantaneous negative potential which the plate can acquire with respect to the cathode without danger of injuring the tube.

Ion. An elementary particle of matter or a small group of such particles having a net positive or negative charge.

Ionization. Process by which ions are produced in solids, liquids, or gases.

Ionization potential. The lowest potential at which ionization takes place within a gas-filled tube.

Ionosphere. A region composed of highly ionized layers of atmosphere from 70 to 250 miles above the surface of the earth.

Kilo (k). A prefix meaning 1,000.

Kilocycle (kc). One thousand cycles; conversationally used to indicate 1,000 cycles per second.

Klystron. A tube in which oscillations are generated by the bunching of electrons (that is, velocity modulation). This tube utilizes the transit time between two given electrodes to deliver pulsating energy to a cavity resonator in order to sustain oscillations within the cavity.

Lag. The amount one wave is behind another in time; expressed in electrical degrees.

Lead The opposite of *lag.* Also, a wire or connection.

Leakage. The electrical loss due to poor insulation.

Lecher line. A section of open-wire transmission line used for measurements of standing waves.

Limiting. Removal by electronic means of one or both extremities of a waveform at a predetermined level.

Linear. Having an output which varies in direct proportion to the input.

Line-balance converter. A device used at the end of a coaxial line to isolate the outer conductor from ground.

Load. The impedance to which energy is being supplied.

Local oscillator. The oscillator used in a superheterodyne receiver the output of which is mixed with the desired r-f carrier to form the intermediate frequency.

Loose coupling. Less than critical coupling; coupling providing little transfer of energy.

Magnetic circuit. The complete path of magnetic lines of force.

Magnetic field (H). The space in which a magnetic force exists.

Magnetron. A vacuum-tube oscillator containing two electrodes, in which the flow of electrons from cathode to anode is controlled by an externally applied magnetic field.

Matched impedance. The condition which exists when two coupled circuits are so adjusted that their impedances are equal.

Meg (mega) (m). A prefix meaning one million.

Megacycle (M_c). One million cycles. Used conversationally to mean 1,000,000 cycles per second.

Metallic insulator. A shorted quarter-wave section of a transmission line which acts as an electrical insulator at a frequency corresponding to its quarter-wave length.

Mho. The unit of conductance.

Micro (μ). A prefix meaning one-millionth.

Microsecond (μs). One-millionth of a second.

Milli (m). A prefix meaning one-thousandth.

Milliampera (ma). One-thousandth of an ampere.

Mixer. A vacuum tube or crystal and suitable circuit used to combine the incoming and local-oscillator frequencies to produce an intermediate frequency. *See* Beat frequency.

Modulation. The process of varying the amplitude (amplitude modulation), the frequency (frequency modulation), or the phase (phase modulation) of a carrier wave in accordance with other signals in order to convey intelligence. The modulating signal may be an audiofrequency signal, video signal (as in television), or electrical pulses or tones to operate relays, etc.

Modulator. The circuit which provides the signal that varies the ampli- tude, frequency, or phase of the oscillations generated in the transmitter tube.

Multielectrode tube. A vacuum tube containing more than three electrodes associated with a single electron stream.

Multiunit tube. A vacuum tube containing within one envelope two or more groups of electrodes, each associated with separate electron streams.

Multivibrator. A type of relaxation oscillator for the generation of nonsinusoidal waves in which the output of each of its two tubes is coupled to the input of the other to sustain oscillations.

Mutual conductance (g_m). *See* Transconductance.

Mutual inductance. A circuit property existing when the relative position of two inductors causes the magnetic lines of force from one to link with the turns of the other.

Negative feedback. *See* Degeneration.

Neon bulb. A glass bulb containing two electrodes in neon gas at low pressure.

Network. Any electrical circuit containing two or more interconnected elements.

Neutralisation. The process of nullifying the voltage fed back through the interelectrode capacitance of an amplifier tube, by providing an equal voltage of opposite phase; generally necessary only with triode tubes.

Node. A zero point; specifically, a current node is a point of zero current and a voltage node is a point of zero voltage.

Noninductive capacitor. A capacitor in which the inductive effects at high frequencies are reduced to the minimum.

Noninductive circuit. A circuit in which inductance is reduced to a minimum or negligible value.

Nonlinear. Having an output which does not vary in direct proportion to the input.

Ohm (ω). The unit of electrical resistance.

Open circuit. A circuit which does not provide a complete path for the flow of current.

Optimum coupling. See Critical coupling.

Oscillator. A circuit capable of converting direct current into alternating current of a frequency determined by the constants of the circuit. It generally uses a vacuum tube.

Oscillatory circuit. A circuit in which oscillations can be generated or sustained.

Oscillograph. See Oscilloscope.

Oscilloscope. An instrument for showing, visually, graphical representations of the waveforms encountered in electrical circuits.

Overdriven amplifier. An amplifier designed to distort the input signal waveform by a combination of cut-off limiting and saturation limiting.

Overload. A load greater than the rated load of an electrical device.

Parallel feed. Application of a d-c voltage to the plate or grid of a tube in parallel with an a-c circuit so that the d-c and a-c components flow in separate paths. Also called shunt feed.

Parallel-resonant circuit. A resonant circuit in which the applied voltage is connected across a parallel circuit formed by a capacitor and an inductor.

Paraphase amplifier. An amplifier which converts a single input into a push-pull output.

Parasitic suppressor. A resistor in a vacuum-tube circuit to prevent un-wanted oscillations.

Peaking circuit. A type of circuit which converts an input to a peaked output waveform.

Peak plate current. The maximum instantaneous plate current passing through a tube.

Peak value. The maximum instantaneous value of a varying current, voltage, or power. It is equal to 1.414 times the effective value of a sine wave.

Pentode. A five-electrode vacuum tube containing a cathode, control, grid, screen grid, suppressor grid, and plate.

Phase difference. The time in electrical degrees by which one wave leads or lags another.

Phase inversion. A phase difference of 180 between two similar waveshapes of the same frequency.

Phase-splitting circuit. A circuit which produces from the same input waveform two output waveforms which differ in phase from each other.

Phosphorescence. The property of emitting light for some time after excitation by electronic bombardment.

Piezoelectric effect. The effect of producing a voltage by placing a stress, either by compression, by expansion, or by twisting, on a crystal, and, conversely, the effect of producing a stress in a crystal by applying a voltage to it.

Plate (P). The principal electrode in a tube to which the electron stream is attracted. See Anode.

Plate circuit. The complete electrical circuit connecting the cathode and plate of a vacuum tube.

Plate current (i_p). The current flowing in the plate circuit of a vacuum tube.

Plate detection. The operation of a vacuum-tube detector at or near cutoff so that the input signal is rectified in the plate circuit.

Plate dissipation. The power in watts consumed at the plate in the form of heat.

Plate efficiency. The ratio of the a-c power output from a tube to the average d-c power supplied to the plate circuit.

Plate impedance. See Plate resistance.

Plate-load impedance (R_L or Z_L). The impedance in the plate circuit across which the output signal voltage is developed by the alternating component of the plate current.

Plate modulation. Amplitude modulation of a class-C r-f amplifier by varying the plate voltage in accordance with the signal.

Plate resistance (r_p). The internal resistance to

the flow of alternating current between the cathode and plate of tube. It is equal to a small change in plate voltage divided by the corresponding change in plate current, and is expressed in ohms. It is also called a-c resistance, internal impedance, plate impedance, and dynamic plate impedance. The static plate resistance, or resistance to the flow of *direct current* is a different value. It is denoted by R_p.

Positive feedback. See Regeneration.

Potentiometer. A variable voltage divider; a resistor which has a variable contact arm so that any portion of the potential applied between its ends may be selected.

Power. The rate of doing work or the rate of expending energy. The unit of electrical power is the watt.

Power amplification. The process of amlifying a signal to produce a gain in power, as distinguished from voltage amplification. The gain in the ratio of the alternating power output to the alternating power input of an amplifier.

Power factor. The ratio of the actual power of an alternating or pulsating current, as measured by a wattmeter, to the apparent power, as indicated by ammeter and voltmeter readings. The power factor if an inductor, capacitor, or insulator is an expression of the losses.

Power tube. A vacuum tube designed to handle a greater amount of power than the ordinary voltage-amplifying tube.

Primary circuit. The first, in electrical order, of two or more coupled circuits, in which a change in current induces a voltage in the other or secondary circuits; such as the primary winding of a transformer.

Propagation. See Wave propagation.

Pulsating current. A unidirectional current which increases and decreases in magnitude.

Push-pull circuit. A push-pull circuit usually refers to an amplifier circuit using two vacuum tubes in such a fashion that when one vacuum tube is operating on a positive alternation, the other vacuum tube operates on a negative alternation.

Q. The figure of merit of efficiency of a circuit or coil. Numerically it is equal to the inductive reactance divided by the resistance of the circuit or coil.

Radiate. To send out energy, such as r-f waves, into space.

Radiation resistance. A fictitious resistance which may be considered to dissipate the energy radiated from the antenna.

Radio frequency (r-f). Any frequency of electrical energy capable of propagation into space. Radio frequencies normally are much higher than sound-wave frequencies.

Radio-frequency amplification. The amplification of a radio wave by a receiver before detection, or by a transmitter before radiation.

Radio-frequency choke (RFC). An air-core or powdered iron core coil used to impede the flow of r-f currents.

Radio-frequency component. See Carrier.

Ratio. The value obtained by dividing one number by another, indicating their relative proportions.

Reactance (X). The opposition offered to the flow of an alternating current by the inductance, capacitance, or both, in any circuit.

Reciprocal. The value obtained by dividing the number 1 by any quantity.

Rectifier. A device used to change alternating current to unidirectional current.

Reflected impedance. See Coupled impedance.

Reflection. The turning back of a radio wave caused by reradiation from any conducting surface which is large in comparison to the wavelength of the radio wave.

Reflector. A metallic object placed behind a radiating antenna to prevent r-f radiation in an undesired direction and to reinforce radiation in a desired direction.

Regeneration. The process of returning a part of the output signal of an amplifier to its input circuit in such a manner that it reinforces the grid excitation and thereby increases the total amplification.

Regulation (voltage). The ratio of the change in voltage due to a load to the open-circuit voltage, expressed in per cent.

Relaxation oscillator. A circuit for the generation of nonsinusoidal waves by gradually storing and quickly releasing energy either in the electric field of a capacitor or in the magnetic field of an inductor.

Reluctance. The opposition to magnetic flux.

Resistance (R). The opposition to the flow of current caused by the nature and physical dimensions of a conductor.

Resistor. A circuit element whose chief characteristic is resistance; used to oppose the flow of current.

Resonance. The condition existing in a circuit in which the inductive and capacitive reactances cancel.

Resonance curve. A graphical representation of the manner in which a resonant circuit responds to various frequencies at and near the resonant frequency.

Rheostat. A variable resistor.

Ripple voltage. The fluctuations in the output voltage of a rectifier, filter, or generator.

rms. Abbreviation of root mean square. See Effective value.

Saturation. The condition existing in any circuit when an increase in the driving signal produces no further change in the resultant effect.

Saturation limiting. Limiting the minimum output voltage of a vacuum-tube circuit by operating the tube in the region of plate-current saturation (not to be confused with emission saturation).

Saturation point. The point beyond which an increase in either grid voltage, plate voltage, or both produces no increase in the existing plate current.

Screen dissipation. The power dissipated in the form of heat on the screen grid as the result of bombardment by the electron stream.

Screen grid (S_c). An electrode placed between the control grid and the plate of a vacuum tube to reduce interelectrode capacitance.

Secondary. The output coil of a transformer. See Primary circuit.

Secondary emission. The emission of electrons knocked loose from the plate, grid, or fluorescent screen of a vacuum tube by the impact or bombardment of electrons arriving from the cathode.

Selectivity. The degree to which a receiver is capable of discriminating between signals of different carrier frequencies.

Self-bias. The bias of a tube created by the voltage drop developed across a resistor through which either its cathode current or its grid current flows.

Self-excited oscillator. An oscillator depending on its resonant circuits for frequency determination. See Crystal oscillator.

Self-induction. The production of a counter-electromotive force in a conductor when its own magnetic field collapses or expands with a change in current in the conductor.

Sensitivity. The degree of response of a circuit to signals of the frequency to which it is tuned.

Series feed. Application of the d-c voltage to the plate or grid of a tube through the same impedance in which the alternating current flows. Compare *Parallel feed.*

Series resonance. The condition existing in a circuit when the source of voltage is in series with an inductor and capacitor whose reactances cancel each other at the applied frequency and thus reduce the impedance to a minimum.

Series-resonant circuit. A resonant circuit in which the capacitor and the inductor are in series with the applied voltage.

Shielding. A metallic covering used to prevent magnetic or electrostatic coupling between adjacent circuits.

Short-circuit. A low-impedance or zero-impedance path between two points.

Shunt. Parallel. A parallel resistor placed in an ammeter to increase its range.

Shunt feed. See Parallel feed. *Sine wave.* The curve traced by the projection on a uniform time scale of the end of a rotating arm, or vector. Also known as a sinusoidal wave.

Skin effect. The tendency of alternating currents to flow near the surface of a conductor, thus being restricted to a small part of the total cross-sectional area. This effect increases the resistance and becomes more marked as the frequency rises.

Soft tube. A vacuum tube the characteristics of which are adversely affected by the presence of gas in the tube; not to be confused with tubes designed to operate with gas inside them.

Solenoid. A multiturn coil of wire wound in a

uniform layer or layerson a hollow cylindrical form.

Space charge. The cloud of electrons existing in the space between the cathode and plate in a vacuum tube, formed by the electrons emitted from the cathode in excess of those immediately attracted to the plate.

Space current. The total current flowing between the cathode and all the other electrodes in a tube. This includes the plate current, grid current, screen-grid current, and any other electrode current which may be present.

Stability. Freedom from undesired variation.

Standing wave. A distribution of current and voltage on a transmission line formed by two sets of waves traveling in opposite directions, and characterized by the presence of a number of points of successive maxima and minima in the distribution curves.

Static. A fixed nonvarying condition; without motion.

Static characteristics. The characteristics of a tube with no output load and with d-c potentials applied to the grid and plate.

Superheterodyne. A receiver in which the incoming signal is mixed with a locally generated signal to produce a predetermined intermediate frequency.

Suppressor grid (Su). An electrode used in a vacuum tube to minimize the harmful effects of secondary emission from the plate.

Surge. Sudden changes of current or voltage in a circuit.

Surge impedance (Co). See Characteristic impedance.

Sweep circuit. *The part of a cathode-ray oscilloscope which provides a time-reference base.*

Swing. The variation in frequency or amplitude of an electrical quantity.

Swinging choke. A choke with an effective inductance which varies with the amount of current passing through it. It is used in some power-supply filter circuits.

Synchronous. Happening at the same time; having the same period and phase.

Tank circuit. See Parallel-resonant circuit.

Tetrode. A four-electrode vacuum tube containing a cathode, control grid, screen grid, and plate.

Thermionic emission. Electron emission caused by heating an emitter.

Thermocouple ammeter. An ammeter which operates by means of a voltage produced by the heating effect of a current passed through the junction of two dissimilar metals. It is used for r-f measurements.

Thyratron. A hot-cathode, gas-discharge tube in which one or more electrodes are used to control electrostatically the starting of an unidirectional flow of current.

Tight coupling. Degree of coupling in which practically all of the magnetic lines of force produced by one coil link a second coil.

Trace. A visible line or lines appearing on the screen of a cathode-ray tube in operation.

Transconductance (G_m). The ratio of the change in plate current to the change in grid voltage producing this change in plate current, while all other electrode voltages remain constant.

Transformer. A device composed of two or more coils, linked by magnetic lines of force, used to transfer energy from one circuit to another.

Transient. The voltage or current which exists as the result of a change from one steady-state condition to another.

Transit time. The time which electrons take to travel between the cathode and the plate of a vacuum tube.

Transmission lines. Any conductor or system of conductors used to carry electrical energy from its source to a load.

Triggering. Starting an action in another circuit, which then functions for a time under its own control.

Triode. A three-electrode vacuum tube, containing a cathode, control grid, and plate.

Tuned circuit. A resonant circuit.

Tuning. The process of adjusting a radio circuit so that it resonates at the desired frequency.

Unbalanced line. A transmission line in which the voltages on the two conductors are not equal with respect to ground; for example, a coaxial line.

Unidirectional. In one direction only.

Vacuum-tube voltmeter (VTVM). A device which uses either the amplifier characteristic or the rectifier characteristic of a vacuum tube or both to measure either d-c or a-c voltages. Its input impedance is very high, and the current used to actuate the meter movement is not taken from the circuit being measured. It can be used to obtain accurate measurements in sensitive circuits.

Variable-u tube. A vacuum tube in which the control grid is irregularly spaced, so that the grid exercises a different amount of control on the electron stream at different points within its operating range.

Variocoupler. Two independent inductors, so arranged mechanically that their mutual inductance (coupling) can be varied.

Variometer. A variocoupler having its two coils connected in series, and so mounted that the movable coil may be rotated within the fixed coil, thus changing the total inductance of the unit.

Vector. A line used to represent both direction and magnitude.

Velocity modulation. A method of modulation in which the input signal voltage is used to change the velocity of electrons in a constant-current electron beam so that the electrons are grouped into bunches.

Video amplifier. A circuit capable of amplifying a very wide range of frequencies, including and exceeding the audio band of frequencies.

Volt (V). The unit of electrical potential.

Voltage amplification. The process of amplifying a signal to produce a gain in voltage. The voltage gain of an amplifier is the ratio of its alternating-voltage output to its alternating-voltage input.

Voltage divider. An impedance connected across a voltage source. The load is connected across a fraction of this impedance so that the load voltage is substantially in proportion to this fraction.

Voltage doubler. A method of increasing the voltage by rectifying both halves of a cycle and causing the outputs of both halves to be additive.

Voltage regulation. A measure of the degree to which a power source maintains its output-voltage stability under varying load conditions.

Watt (w). The unit of electrical power.

Wave. Loosely, an electromagnetic impulse, periodically changing in intensity and traveling through space. More specifically, the graphical representation of the intensity of that impulse over a oeriod of time.

Waveform. The shape of the wave obtained when instantaneous values of an a-c quantity are plotted againsi: time in rectangular coordinates.

Wavelength (A). The distance, usually expressed in meters, traveled by a wave during the time interval of one complete cycle. It is equal to the velocity divided by the frequency.

Wave propagation. The transmission of r-f energy through space.

Wien-bridge circuit. A circuit in which the various values of capacitance and resistance are made to balance with each other at a certain frequency.

X. The symbol for reactance.

Z. The symbol for impedance.

ELECTRONICS SYMBOLS

AMPLIFIER (2)

general

with two inputs

with two outputs

with adjustable gain

with associated power supply

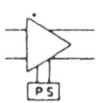

with associated attenuator

with external feedback path

Amplifier Letter Combinations (amplifier-use identification in symbol if required)

BDG	Bridging
BST	Booster
CMP	Compression
DC	Direct Current
EXP	Expansion
LIM	Limiting
MON	Monitoring
PGM	Program
PRE	Preliminary
PWR	Power
TRQ	Torque

ANTENNA (3)

general

dipole

loop

counterpoise

ARRESTER, LIGHTNING (4)

general

carbon block

electrolytic or aluminum cell

horn gap

protective gap

sphere gap

valve or film element

multigap

ATTENUATOR, FIXED (see PAD) (57) (same symbol as variable attenuator, without variability)

ATTENUATOR, VARIABLE (5)

balanced

unbalanced

AUDIBLE SIGNALING DEVICE (6)

bell, electrical; ringer, telephone

buzzer

horn, electrical; loudspeaker; siren; underwater sound hydrophone, projector or transducer

Horn, Letter Combinations (if required)

*HN	Horn, electrical	
*HW	Howler	
*LS	Loudspeaker	
*SN	Siren	
‡EM	Electromagnetic with moving coil	
‡EMN	Electromagnetic with moving coil and neutralizing winding	
‡MG	Magnetic armature	
‡PM	Permanent magnet with moving coil	

identification replaces (*) asterisk and (‡) dagger)

sounder, telegraph

BATTERY (7)

generalized direct current source; one cell

multicell

CAPACITOR (8)

general

polarized

adjustable or variable

continuously adjustable or variable differential

phase-shifter

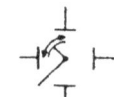

split-stator

feed-through

CELL, PHOTOSENSITIVE (Semiconductor) (9)

asymmetrical photoconductive transducer

symmetrical photoconductive transducer

ELECTRONICS SYMBOLS

photovoltaic transducer; solar cell

CIRCUIT BREAKER (11)

general

with magnetic overload

drawout type

CIRCUIT ELEMENT (12)

general

Circuit Element Letter Combinations (replaces (*) asterisk)

EG	Equalizer
FAX	Facsimile set
FL	Filter
FL-BE	Filter, band elimination
FL-BP	Filter, band pass
FL-HP	Filter, high pass
FL-LP	Filter, low pass
PS	Power supply
RG	Recording unit
RU	Reproducing unit
DIAL	Telephone dial
TEL	Telephone station
TPR	Teleprinter
TTY	Teletypewriter

Additional Letter Combinations (symbols preferred)

AR	Amplifier
AT	Attenuator
C	Capacitor
CB	Circuit breaker
HS	Handset
I	Indicating or switchboard lamp
L	Inductor
J	Jack
LS	Loudspeaker
MIC	Microphone
OSC	Oscillator
PAD	Pad
P	Plug
HT	Receiver, headset
K	Relay
R	Resistor
S	Switch or key switch
T	Transformer
WR	Wall receptacle

CLUTCH; BRAKE (14)

disengaged when operating means is de-energized

engaged when operating means is de-energized

COIL, RELAY and OPERATING (16)

semicircular dot indicates inner end of wiring

CONNECTOR (18)

assembly, movable or stationary portion; jack, plug, or receptacle

jack or receptacle

plug

separable connectors

two-conductor switchboard jack

two-conductor switchboard plug

jacks normalled through one way

jacks normalled through both ways

2-conductor nonpolarized, female contacts

2-conductor polarized, male contacts

waveguide flange

plain, rectangular

choke, rectangular

engaged 4-conductor; the plug has 1 male and 3 female contacts, individual contact designations shown

coaxial, outside conductor shown carried through

coaxial, center conductor shown carried through; outside conductor not carried through

mated choke flanges in rectangular waveguide

COUNTER, ELECTROMAGNETIC; MESSAGE REGISTER (26)

general

with a make contact

COUPLER, DIRECTIONAL (27)
(common coaxial/waveguide usage)

(common coaxial/waveguide usage)

E-plane aperture-coupling, 30-decibel transmission loss

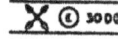

COUPLING (28)

by loop from coaxial to circular waveguide, direct-current grounds connected

CRYSTAL, PIEZO-ELECTRIC (62)

DELAY LINE (31)

general

tapped delay

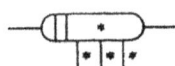

bifilar slow-wave structure (commonly used in traveling-wave tubes)

(length of delay indication replaces (*) asterisk)

DETECTOR, PRIMARY; MEASURING TRANSDUCER (30) (see HALL GENERATOR and THERMAL CONVERTER)

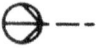

DISCONTINUITY (33) (common coaxial/waveguide usage)

equivalent series element, general

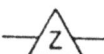

capacitive reactance

inductive reactance

inductance-capacitance circuit, infinite reactance at resonance

ELECTRONICS SYMBOLS

inductance-capacitance circuit, zero reactance at resonance

resistance

equivalent shunt element, general

capacitive susceptance

conductance

inductive susceptance

inductance-capacitance circuit, infinite susceptance at resonance

inductance-capacitance circuit, zero susceptance at resonance

ELECTRON TUBE (34)

triode

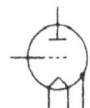

pentode, envelope connected to base terminal

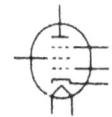

twin triode, equipotential cathode

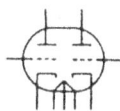

typical wiring figure to show tube symbols placed in any convenient position

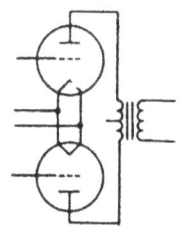

rectifier; voltage regulator (see LAMP, GLOW)

phototube, single and multiplier

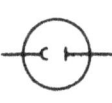 

cathode-ray tube, electrostatic and magnetic deflection

mercury-pool tube, ignitor and control grid (see RECTIFIER)

resonant magnetron, coaxial output and permanent magnet

reflex klystron, integral cavity, aperture coupled

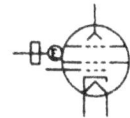

transmit-receive (TR) tube gas filled, tunable integral cavity, aperture coupled, with starter

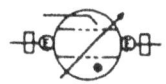

traveling-wave tube (typical)

forward-wave traveling-wave-tube amplifier shown with four grids, having slow-wave structure with attenuation, magnetic focusing by external permanent magnet, rf input and rf output coupling each E-plane aperture to external rectangular waveguide

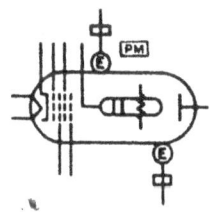

FERRITE DEVICES (100)

field polarization rotator

field polarization amplitude modulator

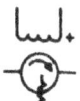

FUSE (36)

high-voltage primary cutout, dry

high-voltage primary cutout, oil

GOVERNOR (Contact-making) (37)

contacts shown here as closed

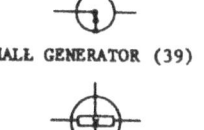

HALL GENERATOR (39)

HANDSET (40)

general

operator's set with push-to talk switch

HYBRID (41)

general

junction (common coaxial/waveguide usage)

circular

(E, H or HE transverse field indicators replace (*) asterisk)

rectangular waveguide and coaxial coupling

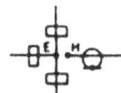

INDUCTOR (42)

general

ELECTRONICS SYMBOLS

magnetic core

tapped

adjustable, continuously adjustable

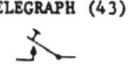

KEY, TELEGRAPH (43)

LAMP (44)

ballast lamp; ballast tube

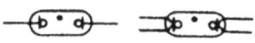

lamp, fluorescent, 2 and 4 terminal

lamp, glow; neon lamp
a-c

d-c

lamp, incandescent

indicating lamp; switchboard lamp
(see VISUAL SIGNALING DEVICE)

LOGIC (see 806B and Y32-14)
(including some duplicate symbols; left and right-hand symbols are not mixed)

AND function

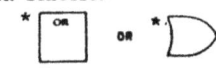

OR function

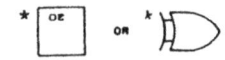

EXCLUSIVE-OR function

((*) input side of logic symbols in general)

condition indicators

state (logic negation)

○

a Logic Negation output becomes 1-state if and only if the input is not 1-state

an AND func. where output is low if and only if all inputs are high

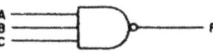

electric inverter

(elec. invtr. output becomes 1-state if and only if the input is 1-state)
(elec. invtr. output is more pos. if and only if input is less pos.)

level (relative)

◁   ◁

1-state is   1-state is
less +   more +

(symbol is a rt. triangle pointing in direction of flow)

an AND func. with input 1-states at more pos. level and output 1-state at less pos. level

single shot (one output)

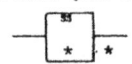

(waveform data replaces inside/outside (*))

schmitt trigger, waveform and two outputs

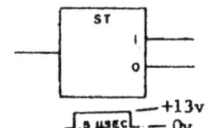

flip-flop, complementary

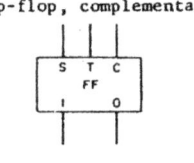

flip-flop, latch

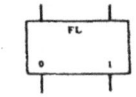

register

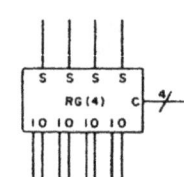

(binary register denoting four flip-flops and bits)

amplifier (see AMPLIFIER)

channel path(s) (see PATH, TRANSMISSION)

magnetic heads (see PICK-UP HEAD)

oscillator (see OSCILLATOR)

relay, contacts (see CONTACT, ELECTRICAL)
relay, electromagnetic (see RELAY COIL RECOGNITION)

signal flow (see DIRECTION OF FLOW)

time delay (see DELAY LINE)

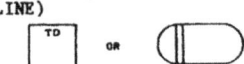

time delay with typical delay taps:

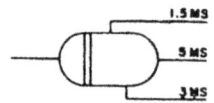

functions not otherwise symbolized

[*]

(identification replaces (*))

Logic Letter Combinations

S	set
C	clear (reset)
T	toggle (trigger)
(N)	number of bits
BO	blocking oscillator
CF	cathode follower
EF	emitter follower
FF	flip-flop
SS	single shot
ST	schmitt trigger
RG(N)	register (N stages)
SR	shift register

MACHINE, ROTATING (46)

generator

motor

METER, INSTRUMENT (48)

(*)

identification replaces (*) asterisk

Meter Letter Combinations

A	Ammeter
AH	Ampere-hour
CMA	Contact-making (or breaking) ammeter
CMC	Contact-making (or breaking) clock
CMV	Contact-making (or breaking) voltmeter
CRO	Oscilloscope or cathode-ray oscillograph
DB	DB (decibel) meter
DBM	DBM (decibels referred to 1 milliwatt) meter
DM	Demand meter
DTR	Demand-totalizing relay
F	Frequency meter
G	Galvanometer
GD	Ground detector
I	Indicating
INT	Integrating
µA or UA	Microammeter
MA	Milliammeter
NM	Noise meter
OHM	Ohmmeter
OP	Oil pressure

ELECTRONICS SYMBOLS

MODE TRANSDUCER (53)

(common coaxial/waveguide usage)

transducer from rectangular waveguide to coaxial with mode suppression, direct-current grounds connected

MOTION, MECHANICAL (54)

rotation applied to a resistor

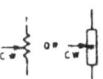

(identification replaces (*) asterisk)

NUCLEAR-RADIATION DETECTOR, gas filled; IONIZATION CHAMBER; PROPORTIONAL COUNTER TUBE; GEIGER-MULLER COUNTER TUBE (50)
(see RADIATION-SENSITIVITY INDICATOR)

PATH, TRANSMISSION (58)

cable; 2-conductor, shield grounded and 3-conductor shielded

PICKUP HEAD (61)

general

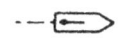

writing; recording

reading; playback

erasing

writing, reading, and erasing

stereo

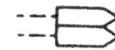

RECTIFIER (65)

semiconductor diode; metallic rectifier; electrolytic rectifier; asymmetrical varistor

mercury-pool tube power rectifier

fullwave bridge-type

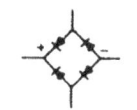

RESISTOR (68)

general

tapped

heating

symmetrical varistor resistor, voltage sensitive (silicon carbide, etc.)

(identification marks replace (*) asterisk)

with adjustable contact

adjustable or continuously adjustable (variable)

(identification replaces (*) asterisk)

RESONATOR, TUNED CAVITY (71)

(common coaxial/waveguide usage)

resonator with mode suppression coupled by an E-plane aperture to a guided transmission path and by a loop to a coaxial path

tunable resonator with direct-current ground connected to an electron device and adjustably coupled by an E-plane aperture to a rectangular waveguide

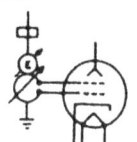

ROTARY JOINT, RF (COUPLER) (72)

general; with rectangular waveguide

(transmission path recognition symbol replaces (*) asterisk)

coaxial type in rectangular waveguide

circular waveguide type in rectangular waveguide

SEMICONDUCTOR DEVICE (73)
(Two Terminal, diode)

semiconductor diode; rectifier

capacitive diode (also Varicap, Varactor, reactance diode, parametric diode)

breakdown diode, unidirectional (also backward diode, avalanche diode, voltage regulator diode, Zener diode, voltage reference diode)

breakdown diode, bidirectional and backward diode (also bipolar voltage limiter)

tunnel diode (also Esaki diode)

temperature-dependent diode

photodiode (also solar cell)

semiconductor diode, PNPN switch (also Shockley diode, four-layer diode and SCR).

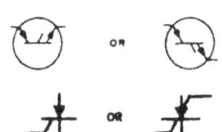

(Multi-Terminal, transistor, etc.)

PNP transistor

NPN transistor

unijunction transistor, N-type base

ELECTRONICS SYMBOLS

unijunction transistor, P-type base

field-effect transistor, N-type base

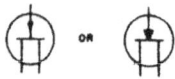

field-effect transistor, P-type base

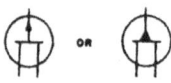

semiconductor triode, PNPN-type switch

semiconductor triode, NPNP-type switch

NPN transistor, transverse-biased base

PNIP transistor, ohmic connection to the intrinsic region

NPIN transistor, ohmic connection to the intrinsic region

PNIN transistor, ohmic connection to the intrinsic region

NPIP transistor, ohmic connection to the intrinsic region

SQUIB (75)

explosive

igniter

sensing link; fusible link operated

SWITCH (76)

push button, circuit closing (make)

push button, circuit opening (break)

nonlocking; momentary circuit closing (make)

nonlocking; momentary circuit opening (break)

transfer

locking, circuit closing (make)

locking, circuit opening (break)

transfer, 3-position

wafer

(example shown: 3-pole 3-circuit with 2 non-shorting and 1 shorting moving contacts)

safety interlock, circuit opening and closing

2-pole field-discharge knife, with terminals and discharge resistor

(identification replaces (*) asterisk)

SYNCHRO (78)

Synchro Letter Combinations
CDX Control-differential transmitter
CT   Control transformer
CX   Control transmitter
TDR Torque-differential receiver
TDX Torque-differential transmitter
TR   Torque receiver
TX   Torque transmitter
RS   Resolver
B   Outer winding rotatable in bearings

THERMAL ELEMENT (83)

actuating device

thermal cutout; flasher

thermal relay

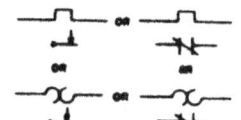

thermostat (operates on rising temperature), contact)

thermostat, make contact

thermostat, integral heater and transfer contacts

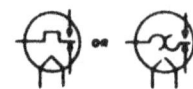

THERMISTOR; THERMAL RESISTOR (84)

with integral heater

THERMOCOUPLE (85)

temperature-measuring

current-measuring, integral heater connected

current-measuring, integral heater insulated

temperature-measuring, semiconductor

current-measuring, semiconductor

TRANSFORMER (86)

general

magnetic-core

one winding with adjustable inductance

separately adjustable inductance

adjustable mutual inductor, constant-current

ELECTRONICS SYMBOLS

autotransformer, 1-phase adjustable

current, with polarity marking

potential, with polarity mark

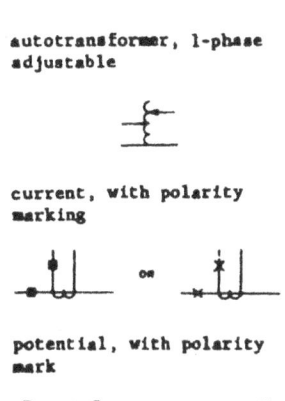

with direct-current connections and mode suppression between two rectangular waveguides
(common coaxial/waveguide usage)

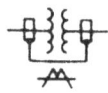

shielded, with magnetic core

with a shield between windings, connected to the frame

VIBRATOR; INTERRUPTER (87)

typical shunt drive (terminals shown)

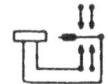

typical separate drive (terminals shown)

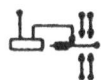

VISUAL SIGNALING DEVICE (88)

communication switchboard-type lamp

indicating, pilot, signaling, or switchboard light (see LAMP)

(identification replaces (*) asterisk)

indicating light letter combinations

A	Amber
B	Blue
C	Clear
G	Green
NE	Neon
O	Orange
OP	Opalescent
P	Purple
R	Red
W	White
Y	Yellow

jeweled signal light

TRANSISTOR SYMBOLS

Semiconductor, General
BV............Breakdown voltage
TA .... Ambient temperature
T_{ep}............ Operating temperature

Transistor
B, b...........Base electrode
C, c...........Collector electrode
C_{ib} ....Input capacitance (common base)
C_{ie} ....Input capacitance (common emitter)
C_{ob}..........Output capacitance (common base)
C_{oe}..........Output capacitance (common emitter)
E, e...........Emitter electrode
I_B..............Base current (dc)
i_b..............Base current (instantaneous)
I_C..............Collector current (dc)
i_c..............Collector current (instantaneous)
I_{CBO} ....Collector cutoff current (dc) emitter open
I_{CEO}..........Collector cutoff current (dc) base open
I_E ....Emitter current
R_B ....External base resistance
r_b. ....Base spreading resistance
r_i ....Input junction resistance
V_{BB} ....Base supply voltage
V_c...............Collector voltage (with respect to ground or common point)
V_{BE} .... Base to emitter voltage (dc)
V_{CB} ....Collector to base voltage (dc)
V_{CE}..........Collector to emitter voltage (dc)
V_{ce}............Collector to emitter voltage (rms)
vce .... Collector to emitter voltage (instantaneous)
V_{CE} (sat) ....Collector to emitter saturation voltage
v_{EBO} ....Emitter to base voltage (static)
v_{CC} ....Collector supply voltage
V_{EE}...........Emitter supply voltage

TUBE SYMBOLS

A_{hf}	High frequency gain
A_{lf}	Low frequency gain
A_v	Voltage gain
C_c	Coupling capacitor
C_d	Distributed capacitance
C_{gk}	Grid-to-cathode capacitance
C_{gp}	Grid-to-plate capacitance
C_i	Input capacitance
C_K	Cathode bypass capacitor
C_O	Output capacitance
C_{pk}	Plate-to-cathode capacitance
C_s	Shunt capacitance ($C_d + C_i + C_o$)
E_b	Plate volts (dc)
E_{bb}	Supply volts (dc)
E_{bo}	Quiescent plate voltage
E_{c1}	Control grid voltage
E_{c2}	Screen grid voltage
E_{cc}	Control grid supply voltage
E_f	Filament terminal voltage
e_b	Instantaneous total plate volts (ac and dc)
e_{c1}	Instantaneous total control grid volts (ac and dc)
e_{c2}	Instantaneous total screen grid volts (ac and dc)
e_{g1}	Instantaneous value of ac control grid volts
e_{g2}	Instantaneous value of ac screen grid volts
e_{po}	Instantaneous value of plate voltage above and below the quiescent value
E_g	RMS value of grid volts
E_p	RMS value of plate volts
g_m	Grid-plate transconductance (mutual conductance)
I_b	DC value of plate volts
I_{bo}	Quiescent value of plate current
I_{c1}	DC value of control grid current
I_{C2}	DC value of screen grid current
I_f	Filament or heater current
I_{g1}	RMS value of control grid current
I_{g2}	RMS value of screen grid current
I_{gml}	Crest values of ac current control grid
g_{m2}	Crest values of ac current screen grid
I_p	RMS values of plate current
I_{pm}	Crest value of plate current
I_s	Total electron emission
i_b	Instantaneous total value of plate current
i_{c1}	Instantaneous total value of control grid current
i_{c2}	Instantaneous total value of screen grid current
i_{g1}	Instantaneous ac value of control grid current
i_{g2}	Instantaneous ac value of screen grid current
i_p	Instantaneous ac value of plate current
i_{po}	Instantaneous values of plate current above and below the quiescent value
R_b	DC plate resistance
R_g	DC grid resistance
R_k	DC cathode resistance
R_L	Plate load resistance
r_p	AC plate resistance
μ	Amplification factor

www.ingramcontent.com/pod-product-compliance
Lightning Source LLC
Chambersburg PA
CBHW081820300426
44116CB00014B/2434